The Joy of Blueberries Cookbook

Nature's Little Blue Powerhouse

by Theresa Millang

Adventure Publications, Inc.
Cambridge, Minnesota

1

A special thank you to all who contributed to this cookbook.

Book and Cover Design by Jonathan Norberg

10 9 8 7 6 5 4
Copyright 2003 by Theresa Nell Millang
Published by Adventure Publications, Inc.
820 Cleveland Street South
Cambridge, MN 55008
1-800-678-7006
www.adventurepublications.net

Printed in China
ISBN-13: 978-1-59193-012-9
ISBN-10: 1-59193-012-X

Table of Contents

Crumbles

Strudels

Cakes

Coffee Cakes

Other Desserts

Muffins

Pancakes and Waffles

Breads

Salads and Soups

Beverage and Miscellaneous

Introduction

When I became aware of the great health benefits of blueberries, I knew I had to do a cookbook. I began by collecting information on blueberries. There were many interesting articles in national magazines, health magazines and on the web.

I love blueberries in any form. I began collecting, sorting and testing recipes. I was pleasantly surprised to find so many ways to use blueberries. I also found that people were very interested in the health benefits of blueberries and were very willing to share their favorite recipes.

Having done books on muffins, pies, brownies and cheesecakes, I know the importance of variety. Many of my recipes incorporate other fruits (fresh, frozen or canned), such as apple, pineapple, apricot, raspberry, peach or cranberry. I present in this cookbook categories featuring cobblers, crisps, muffins, trail mix, smoothies, pies, cakes, dessert wraps, bars, salads, toaster pastries, breads, punch, toppings, tortes, waffles and so much more.

So, enjoy, and reap the health benefits in every recipe!

Everyone's Talking About the Benefits of Blueberries

Recent studies at the USDA Human Nutrition Research Center on Aging at Tufts University rank blueberries as the greatest antioxidant powerhouse out of 40 fresh fruits, juices and vegetables tested. Antioxidants scavenge for oxygen free radicals, which are thought to cause or accelerate many of the health problems associated with aging. When free radicals build to toxic levels in our bodies, this is known as oxidative stress. Toxic levels of free radicals have been blamed for cell damage that causes cancer, heart disease and age-related disorders.

The good news is that flavorful and versatile blueberries absorb more of these damaging free radicals than other fruits and vegetables. The plant chemical anthocyanin, which causes the dark blue color of the berries, is thought to be responsible for the super antioxidant power of blueberries. Dr. Richard Prior, director of studies at the USDA Human Nutrition Research Center on Aging at Tufts University, states that just one-half cup of blueberries can nearly double the amount of antioxidants most people consume in one day.

Blueberries show great capability in warding off, and even reversing, inward and outward effects of aging. In addition, blueberries are effective in fighting urinary tract infections, warding off wrinkles and varicose veins, reducing the risk of heart disease and cancer, lowering "bad cholesterol" (LDL) levels, supporting good vision and increasing overall capillary elasticity and health for better circulation. In studies funded by the National Institute on Aging and the USDA, antioxidants were found to prevent some age-related motor changes and short-term memory loss. Blueberries are also a good source of dietary fiber and Vitamin C.

Blueberries have remarkable health potential, plus they're delicious. Enjoy and spread the word!

Sources:

"Blueberries: New Thrills for Those Over the Hill." *World Disease Weekly Plus*, Sept 27 (1999): NA.

Keville, Kathy. "Taking Food to Heart." *Better Nutrition* 63 (Sept. 2001): 54.

McCord, Holly. "The Miracle Berry." *Prevention* 51 (June 1999): 122.

"Researching a Blueberry/Brain Power Connection." *Tufts University Health & Nutrition Letter* 19 (March 2001): 4.

Tyler, Varro E. "The Miracle of Anti-Aging Herbs." *Prevention* 51 (Nov. 1999): 105.

Tips for Vibrant Health and Beauty at Every Age. "The Benefits of Blueberries." *Saturday Evening Post* 273 (Sept. 2001): 30.

"What to Eat to Prevent Wrinkles: Ward off Laugh Lines and Other Wrinkles with These Five Foods." *Natural Health* 32 (April 2002): 26.

Facts and Tips

Blueberries, so named because of their deep blue color, are also known as bilberries, whortleberries and hurtleberries. They are often confused with huckleberries. Blueberries were picked by hand until the development of the blueberry rake, which was invented in Maine, the blueberry state, in 1822. The most popular variety is known as the highbush blueberry. The wild lowbush blueberries are a favorite with those who enjoy picking their own.

Selection and Storage

Choose blueberries that are blue all over and are firm and dry—those with greenish-white spots on the bottom are not ripe. Store the fresh blueberries, unwashed, in the refrigerator, and use within ten days of purchase. Wash just before serving. Freeze blueberries unwashed in a plastic food bag. Wash just before using—this dry packing method allows the blueberries to freeze individually—washing before freezing will lump them together. You can wash the blueberries before freezing if desired. If washed, dry and freeze one layer at a time on a cookie sheet before bagging for the freezer—this works well.

Facts

Fresh, frozen or dried blueberries have the same nutritional value.
Blueberries are number one in antioxidant power in fruits and vegetables.
Blueberries contain about 83 calories per 1 cup serving, fresh or frozen.
Blueberries are available year-round and are easy to use: no peeling, coring, etc.

Blueberry Harvest Begins

Florida, April 1st
Louisiana and North Carolina, May 15th
Georgia, New Jersey and Oregon, June 1st
Maine, Michigan, Indiana, British Columbia and Canada, July 1st
Harvest will usually continue until mid-October.

Planting Blueberry Bushes

Soil
Blueberries can be successfully grown in many different kinds of soil. However, a well-drained soil with high organic matter is the best. Soil samples should be taken well in advance to check the pH level and other nutrients, so the adjustments can be made, if required, before planting.

Blueberry bushes require acidic soil (pH of 4.5 to 5.5) with a high content of organic material to maintain moisture. Sand, organic or peat soils loose in texture are preferred. Blueberry plants can be grown in acidic clay soil. This may be accomplished by mixing quantities of peat with clay in a hole the size of a bushel, and planting the bush into this mixture. If you do not know your soil's pH, you can get it tested (for a small fee) by a lab or your local Agriculture Department. If your soil's pH is above 5.5, you can acidify it by adding sulfur.

Watering
Constant but moderate moisture supplied throughout the growing season is required. Overwatering for long periods is not good. If the first inch of soil has moisture, then do not water. If maintaining moisture is a problem, you can put a mulch on top of the soil. Use leaf mold or well-rotted sawdust compost or other good mulching materials—do not use cedar.

A drip irrigation system can be installed, but overhead irrigation is more commonly used and preferred.

Spacing
Blueberry bushes should be planted in rows, with 3½ feet between plants, depending on the variety. If you plan on planting large areas, the rows should be 10 feet apart.

Crisps
Cobblers
Buckles
Crumbles
Strudels

APRICOT-BLUEBERRY CRISP

Fresh, frozen or canned fruit may be used in this crisp.

Filling
2 cups diced canned apricots, drained
2 cups frozen blueberries
¼ cup chopped dried apricots
¼ cup granulated sugar
1 teaspoon pure vanilla extract

Topping
1 cup all-purpose flour
⅓ cup quick-cooking oatmeal, uncooked
¼ cup brown sugar, packed; ¼ cup granulated sugar
½ teaspoon ground cinnamon
⅛ teaspoon ground nutmeg
¼ teaspoon salt
7 tablespoons butter, melted and cooled

vanilla ice cream

Preheat oven to 350°.
In a bowl, mix all filling ingredients; spoon into a well-buttered 8-inch square glass baking dish.

In another bowl, mix all topping ingredients except butter. Stir in butter a little at a time until a moist crumbly mixture is formed; top fruit evenly with mixture. Bake until bubbly and topping is browned, about 45 minutes. Serve warm, topped with vanilla ice cream as desired.

Makes 8 servings.

FRESH BLUEBERRY CRISP

Splashed with fresh lemon juice, and topped with brown sugar, ground cinnamon and oats.

Filling
5 cups fresh blueberries
1 tablespoon fresh lemon juice
1 teaspoon pure vanilla extract

Topping
¾ cup brown sugar, packed
½ cup all-purpose flour
½ teaspoon ground cinnamon
¾ cup oatmeal, uncooked
¼ cup cold butter, cut up

Preheat oven to 375°.
Spread blueberries evenly onto bottom of a lightly greased 13x9-inch glass baking dish. Mix lemon juice and vanilla in a small bowl; sprinkle evenly over blueberries.

In a bowl, mix all topping ingredients. Sprinkle evenly over blueberries. Bake 35–40 minutes. Serve warm with vanilla ice cream.

Makes 10 servings.

GRANOLA-TOPPED BLUEBERRY CRISP

Coconut, ground cinnamon and granola tops this crisp.

Filling
4 cups fresh or frozen blueberries
¼ cup granulated sugar
¼ teaspoon ground cinnamon
1 tablespoon fresh lemon juice
1 teaspoon pure vanilla extract

Topping
1½ cups granola
⅓ cup flaked coconut
2 tablespoons butter, melted

Preheat oven to 375°.
Place blueberries in a large bowl. Mix sugar and cinnamon in a small bowl; stir into blueberries. Stir in lemon juice and vanilla. Pour mixture into a buttered 10x7-inch or similar size baking pan.

In a bowl, mix all topping ingredients until well blended. Sprinkle evenly over blueberry mixture. Bake 35–40 minutes. Serve warm.

Makes 6 servings.

LAYERED BLUEBERRY CRISP

A flavorful graham cracker-layered blueberry crisp.

1 cup graham cracker crumbs
¼ cup butter, melted
1 tablespoon granulated sugar
4 cups fresh blueberries, divided
¾ cup brown sugar, packed
1 teaspoon ground cinnamon
¼ teaspoon ground nutmeg
⅛ teaspoon ground cloves
½ teaspoon salt
1 teaspoon pure vanilla extract
2 tablespoons fresh lemon juice, divided
1 tablespoon water

Preheat oven to 350°.
Mix first three ingredients. Press ⅓ cup mixture onto bottom of a 2-quart baking dish. Sprinkle 2 cups blueberries evenly over crumbs.

Mix brown sugar, spices and salt. Stir in vanilla. Sprinkle ½ brown sugar mixture over blueberries. Sprinkle with 1 tablespoon lemon juice and water. Repeat layers with ⅓ cup crumbs, remaining blueberries, brown sugar mixture and lemon juice. Top with remaining ⅓ cup crumbs. Cover and bake 40 minutes. Increase heat to 400°. Bake another 10 minutes. Serve warm, topped with sweetened whipped cream.

Makes 8 servings.

PECAN-TOPPED BLUEBERRY-APPLE CRISP

Pecans from the Budden grove tops this delicious crisp.

Filling
5 cups fresh blueberries
1 cup apples, peeled, cored and diced
¼ cup granulated sugar
1 teaspoon pure vanilla extract
½ teaspoon freshly grated lemon rind

Topping
½ cup chopped pecans
½ cup all-purpose flour
½ cup quick-cooking oatmeal, uncooked
½ cup brown sugar
1 teaspoon ground cinnamon
½ teaspoon ground nutmeg
¼ teaspoon salt
3 tablespoons butter

Preheat oven to 325°.
Mix all filling ingredients. Spoon mixture into a buttered 8-inch square baking pan; set aside.

Mix all topping ingredients, except butter, until well blended. Add butter; cut in until mixture resembles coarse crumbs. Sprinkle mixture evenly over filling. Bake about 45–50 minutes or until topping is browned. Remove from oven; let stand 10 minutes before serving with vanilla ice cream. Refrigerate leftovers.

Makes 6 to 8 servings.

SAM'S BLUEBERRY-RHUBARB CRISP

Topped with a pistachio crust...like Sam, unforgettable.

Filling
2 cups blueberries
2 cups fresh rhubarb, cut into ½-inch pieces
⅓ cup granulated sugar
2 tablespoons all-purpose flour
1 teaspoon pure vanilla extract

Topping
¾ cup all-purpose flour
½ cup granulated sugar
¼ cup brown sugar, packed
⅛ teaspoon ground nutmeg
6 tablespoons cold butter, cut up
⅓ cup shelled pistachios, finely chopped

Preheat oven to 375°.
Mix first five ingredients. Pour mixture evenly into a lightly buttered 2-quart shallow baking dish.

Mix flour, sugars and nutmeg. Add butter; cut in with a pastry blender until mixture is crumbly. Stir in pistachios until blended. Spoon mixture evenly over filling. Bake 45–50 minutes, until bubbly and topping is crisp. Serve warm.

Makes 8 servings.

BLUEBERRY-PEAR COBBLER

A great summertime treat.

Filling
6 cups sliced fresh pears
1¼ cups fresh blueberries
¾ cup granulated sugar
1 teaspoon pure vanilla extract
¼ cup butter, cut up

Topping
1½ cups all-purpose flour
½ cup cold butter
¼ teaspoon salt
⅛ teaspoon ground nutmeg
2 tablespoons granulated sugar
3 tablespoons cold water
1 egg white, beaten with 1 teaspoon cold water
1 teaspoon granulated sugar, mixed with pinch ground nutmeg

Preheat oven to 425°.
Mix pears, blueberries, sugar and vanilla. Pour mixture into a greased
9-inch square baking pan. Top with cut-up butter.

In a food processor, add butter, flour, salt, nutmeg and sugar. Process on
and off until mixture resembles coarse meal. Add water; process until a
dough forms together. On a floured surface, roll dough out into a square;
place on top of fruit mixture. Make 4 slits on top. Brush with egg mixture;
sprinkle with sugar mixture. Bake about 50 minutes.

Makes 8 servings.

CHOCOLATE BLUEBERRY COBBLER

A favorite with chocolate lovers!

2½ cups blueberries
½ cup raspberries
1 cup granulated sugar, divided
2 tablespoons water
⅓ cup margarine or butter
1 cup all-purpose flour
1 tablespoon baking powder
1 cup whole milk
¼ cup chocolate syrup

Preheat oven to 350°.
Mix berries, ¼ cup sugar and water; let stand a few minutes. Place margarine or butter in a 9-inch square baking pan; melt in oven.

Mix flour, ¾ cup sugar and baking powder. Stir in milk.

Remove pan from oven and pour batter over margarine. Drizzle with chocolate syrup. Spoon berry mixture over top, including liquid. Bake 40–45 minutes or until a toothpick comes out clean. Let stand 10 minutes before serving with vanilla ice cream.

Makes 6 servings.

FRESH BLUEBERRY COBBLER

Top this sweet cobbler with frozen yogurt.

1¼ cups all-purpose flour
½ cup granulated sugar
¼ teaspoon salt
1½ teaspoons baking powder
¾ cup whole milk
⅓ cup butter, melted
3 cups fresh blueberries
⅓ cup granulated sugar
1 teaspoon pure vanilla extract

Preheat oven to 350°.
Mix flour, ½ cup sugar, salt and baking powder. Add milk and butter; stir until combined. Spread batter evenly into a greased 8-inch square baking dish.

Top batter evenly with blueberries. Sprinkle evenly with ⅓ cup sugar and drizzle with vanilla. Bake 40–45 minutes or until a toothpick inserted into the cake portion near the center comes out clean. Serve warm with frozen yogurt.

Makes 10 servings.

LATTICE-CRUSTED
PEACH-BLUEBERRY COBBLER

Serve this lattice-crusted cobbler warm with vanilla ice cream.

Crust
3 cups all-purpose flour
1 teaspoon salt
1 cup solid shortening
6 tablespoons ice cold water, about

Filling
1½ cups granulated sugar
¼ cup cornstarch
1 teaspoon ground cinnamon
¼ teaspoon ground nutmeg
4 cups peeled sliced fresh peaches
3 cups fresh blueberries
1 teaspoon pure vanilla extract
2 tablespoons butter, cut up
1 egg yolk mixed with 1 tablespoon milk

Preheat oven to 375°.
Mix flour and salt. Cut in shortening until mixture resembles coarse crumbs.
Gradually add water, stirring to form a dough. Roll out ⅔ of dough into a
12-inch square. Place into an 8-inch square baking dish; trim even with top
of dish. Roll out remaining dough; cut into 8 1-inch wide strips; set aside.

Mix sugar, cornstarch, cinnamon and nutmeg. Add peaches, blueberries
and vanilla; stir to blend. Pour mixture into prepared crust. Top with butter.
Place the strips of dough over fruit in a lattice form. Brush with egg mixture. Place on baking sheet. Bake about 1 hour.

Makes 8 servings.

MARY DOW'S BLUEBERRY COBBLER

The baking biscuit mix makes this a quick and delicious dessert.

Filling
1 21-ounce can blueberry pie filling
½ teaspoon pure vanilla extract
¼ teaspoon ground cinnamon

Topping
1 cup all-purpose baking biscuit mix
¼ cup whole milk
1 tablespoon butter, softened
2 tablespoons granulated sugar, divided

Preheat oven to 400°.
Mix pie filling, vanilla and cinnamon. Spread mixture into a 1½-quart baking casserole. Heat in oven 7 minutes. Remove from oven.

Mix all topping ingredients except 1 tablespoon sugar. Stir until a soft dough forms. Drop by 6 spoonfuls on top of warm pie filling. Sprinkle with remaining sugar. Bake about 20 minutes, until bubbly and topping is light brown. Serve warm with vanilla ice cream.

Makes 6 servings.

MISTER BROWN'S BLUEBERRY COBBLER

This is an easy dessert to fix on busy days!

Filling
2 21-ounce cans blueberry pie filling
½ teaspoon ground nutmeg
½ teaspoon pure vanilla extract

Topping
1½ cups all-purpose flour
5 tablespoons granulated sugar, divided
1 teaspoon baking powder
½ teaspoon salt
⅓ cup cold butter
3 tablespoons whole milk
1 egg, slightly beaten

Preheat oven to 400°.
Mix pie filling, nutmeg and vanilla. Pour mixture into a 13x9-inch ungreased baking pan.

Mix flour, 2 tablespoons sugar, baking powder and salt. Add butter; cut in with a pastry blender until crumbly. Stir in milk and egg with a fork until just moistened. Spoon mixture over filling and sprinkle with 3 tablespoons sugar. Bake 40–45 minutes. Serve warm with ice cream or plain cream.

Makes 8 servings.

PEACHY BLUEBERRY COBBLER

Serve this juicy cobbler warm with vanilla ice cream.

Filling
1/4 cup brown sugar, firmly packed
1 tablespoon cornstarch
1/2 cup cold water
3 cups peeled and sliced fresh peaches
1 cup fresh blueberries
1 tablespoon butter
1 tablespoon fresh lemon juice
1 teaspoon pure vanilla extract

Topping
1 cup all-purpose flour
1/2 cup granulated sugar
1 1/2 teaspoons baking powder
1/4 cup butter, softened
1/2 cup whole milk
2 tablespoons granulated sugar, mixed with 1/4 teaspoon
    ground cinnamon

Preheat oven to 350°.
In a saucepan, mix sugar and cornstarch; stir in water. Add peaches and blueberries. Cook and stir until thickened and bubbly. Stir in butter, lemon juice and vanilla. Pour into a 1 1/2-quart glass casserole baking dish.

Mix flour, sugar and baking powder. Stir in milk and butter until smooth. Spoon topping in mounds over hot filling and spread evenly. Sprinkle with sugar mixture. Bake about 30–35 minutes or until a wooden pick inserted in topping tests clean.

Makes 6 servings.

HUE'S BLUEBERRY BUCKLE

A nice buckle...serve warm with sweetened whipped cream.

Cake
¾ cup granulated sugar
¼ cup butter
1 large egg
2 cups all-purpose flour
1½ teaspoons baking powder
½ teaspoon salt
¾ cup whole milk
1 teaspoon pure vanilla extract
1½ cups fresh blueberries

Topping
½ cup granulated sugar
⅓ cup all-purpose flour
¾ teaspoon dry pumpkin pie spice
¼ cup butter

Preheat oven to 375°.
Cream ¾ cup sugar and butter. Beat in egg. Mix flour, baking powder and salt; add to creamed mixture. Stir in milk and vanilla until combined. Fold in blueberries. Pour batter evenly into a greased 9-inch square baking pan.

Mix topping ingredients until crumbly. Sprinkle over batter. Bake 45 minutes or until a toothpick inserted near center comes out clean.

Makes 9 servings.

SAUCY PINEAPPLE-BLUEBERRY BUCKLE

Gather the family for this good dessert!

Cake
1¼ cups all-purpose flour
½ cup granulated sugar
¼ cup butter, softened
¼ cup solid shortening
½ cup whole milk
1½ teaspoons baking powder
½ teaspoon salt
1 teaspoon pure vanilla extract
1 egg
1 cup fresh blueberries
1 8-ounce can crushed pineapple
  in syrup, drained; reserve syrup

Topping
½ cup granulated sugar
⅓ cup all-purpose flour
½ teaspoon ground cinnamon
¼ cup butter, softened

Sauce
2 tablespoons brown sugar
1 teaspoon cornstarch
syrup from drained pineapple,
  plus enough water to equal ⅔ cup
¼ teaspoon pure vanilla extract

Preheat oven to 325°.
Mix first nine ingredients; stir in blueberries and drained pineapple. Spread into an ungreased 8-inch square baking pan. Mix all topping ingredients; sprinkle over batter. Bake about 50 minutes or when a wooden pick inserted in center tests clean. Serve with sauce below.

In a saucepan, stir all sauce ingredients except vanilla; bring to a boil. Boil and stir 1 minute. Remove from heat; stir in vanilla. Serve warm.

Makes 8 servings.

EASY BLUEBERRY CRUMBLE

A simple dessert that is simply delicious!

4 cups fresh blueberries
1 cup brown sugar, packed
¾ cup all-purpose flour
¾ cup oatmeal, uncooked
½ cup butter, melted
1 teaspoon pure vanilla extract

Preheat oven to 350°.
Spread blueberries evenly in a 2-quart baking dish.

Mix remaining ingredients; sprinkle over blueberries. Bake 45 minutes.
Serve warm.

Makes 6 servings.

PINEAPPLE-BLUEBERRY CRUMBLE

A cake mix is used in this sweet crumble.

1 18-ounce package yellow cake mix
¾ cup plus 2 tablespoons cold butter, cut up
¾ cup dark brown sugar, firmly packed, divided
½ cup oatmeal, uncooked
1 teaspoon ground cinnamon
1½ cups chopped pecans
2 16-ounce bags frozen unsweetened blueberries
1 20-ounce can crushed pineapple in heavy syrup, undrained
1 teaspoon pure vanilla extract

Preheat oven to 350°.
Mix cake mix, butter, ¼ cup sugar, oatmeal and cinnamon. Blend until mixture resembles coarse meal and holds together in clumps. Add pecans; mix to blend.

Mix blueberries, pineapple, vanilla and remaining sugar. Pour mixture into a buttered 13x9-inch glass baking dish. Spoon cake mix mixture over fruit mixture. Bake until bubbly and topping is brown and crisp, about 1 hour. Serve warm with vanilla ice cream.

Makes 12 servings.

BLUEBERRY STRUDEL

Strudel for that morning cup of coffee!

1 cup butter
2½ cups all-purpose flour
1 cup dairy sour cream
2 cups blueberry jam
6 tablespoons fine dry bread crumbs
¾ cup chopped nuts
¾ cup flaked coconut

Preheat oven to 350°.
In a food processor, process butter and flour to fine crumbs. Add sour cream; mix well. Form a dough; divide into 4 pieces, then form each piece into a 7-inch log shape. Refrigerate 8 hours. Roll each log out into a 10x14-inch rectangle; spread with equal amounts of jam.

Mix bread crumbs, nuts and coconut; sprinkle equal amounts over jam. Roll up like a jelly roll. Place on baking sheets. Bake 50–60 minutes. Cool; cut diagonally into 1-inch widths.

Makes about 40 pieces.

MAPLE-FLAVORED BLUEBERRY-BLACKBERRY STRUDEL

Use the purchased dough for this strudel.

1 cup pure maple syrup
2 cups blueberries
2 cups blackberries
½ teaspoon pure vanilla extract
3 tablespoons cornstarch
2 teaspoons ground cinnamon
2 tablespoons fresh lemon juice
8 sheets phyllo dough, thawed completely
4 tablespoons, melted butter

Preheat oven to 375°.
In a saucepan, mix syrup and berries; cover and simmer 5 minutes over medium-high heat; stir in vanilla. Mix cornstarch, cinnamon and lemon juice; stir into berries. Cook and stir until mixture thickens, about 5 minutes. Remove from heat; cool to room temperature.

Fit a baking sheet with aluminum foil; grease foil all over with margarine or spray with cooking oil spray.

Separate phyllo dough on a dry surface. Add butter to each sheet by dipping a pastry brush into melted butter and adding the butter on each sheet. Restack phyllo sheets. Place filling on short end of stack. Roll, folding in the sides, into a jelly roll shape. Place seam side down on baking sheet. Cut 3 slits through top. Brush with remaining butter. Bake until golden, about 15 minutes.

Makes 10 servings.

Cakes
Coffee Cakes
Shortcakes
Cheesecakes

APPLE-BLUEBERRY BUNDT CAKE

Apples tossed in with blueberries and dried apricots.

½ **cup butter**
1 **cup granulated sugar**
3 **eggs**
2½ **cups all-purpose flour**
1 **tablespoon baking powder**
1 **teaspoon grated orange peel**
½ **teaspoon salt**
½ **cup whole milk, mixed with 1 teaspoon pure vanilla extract**
2 **cups frozen blueberries, partially thawed**
1 **cup peeled, cored and diced apples**
½ **cup dried apricots, diced**
1 **tablespoon all-purpose flour**

Preheat oven to 350°.
In a bowl, beat butter and sugar until fluffy. Beat in eggs one at a time.

Mix 2½ cups flour, baking powder, orange peel and salt. Add flour mixture and milk alternately to creamed mixture. Spread half the batter into a buttered 10-inch tube pan.

Mix blueberries, apples, apricots and 1 tablespoon flour; spoon over batter. Top with remaining batter. Bake about 1 hour or until a wooden pick inserted in center comes out clean. Cool in pan 10 minutes on a rack. Carefully invert cake onto a plate. Serve warm.

Makes 16 servings.

BANANA-BLUEBERRY BUNDT CAKE

Almonds and spice found in this cake.

½ cup slivered almonds
½ cup margarine, softened
1 cup granulated sugar
¼ cup dairy sour cream
1 egg
1 teaspoon pure vanilla extract
3 ripe medium-size bananas, pureed to measure 1½ cups
1 cup blueberries
1¾ cups all-purpose flour
2 teaspoons baking powder
1 teaspoon ground cinnamon
¼ teaspoon ground nutmeg

Preheat oven to 350°.
Sprinkle almonds evenly onto bottom of a greased and floured 10-inch tube pan; set aside.

In a large bowl, beat margarine and sugar until creamy. Add sour cream, egg, vanilla and banana puree; beat until well blended. Stir in blueberries.

Mix flour, baking powder, cinnamon and nutmeg; stir into first bowl until just blended. Pour into prepared pan. Bake 40–45 minutes or until a wooden pick inserted in center comes out clean. Cool in pan 10 minutes. Invert cake onto a plate. Serve warm.

Makes 12 servings.

BEAU'S BLUEBERRY BUNDT CAKE

A quick dessert to prepare for company.

Cake
1 18-ounce box yellow cake mix
¼ cup granulated sugar
3 eggs
1 8-ounce package cream cheese, softened
½ cup corn oil
1 teaspoon pure vanilla extract
1¼ cups blueberries, fresh or frozen

Glaze
1 cup powdered sugar
2 tablespoons orange juice, about
½ teaspoon pure vanilla extract

Preheat oven to 350°.
In a bowl, stir cake mix and sugar. Add eggs, cream cheese, corn oil and vanilla; beat on low until blended, then beat on medium speed 4 minutes. Stir in blueberries by hand. Pour batter into a greased and floured 10-inch bundt pan. Bake 45–55 minutes or until a wooden pick inserted in center comes out clean. Remove from oven; cool in pan 10 minutes. Remove from pan; cool completely on a wire rack.

Mix all glaze ingredients; drizzle over cooled cake.

Makes 16 servings.

BELLE'S PINEAPPLE-BLUEBERRY DUMP CAKE

A special treat adapted from a Whiteville, Louisiana, recipe.

⅔ **cup granulated sugar**
3 tablespoons cornstarch
4 cups fresh or frozen blueberries, divided, or a 21-ounce can
 blueberry pie filling*
2 teaspoons fresh lemon juice
1 teaspoon pure vanilla extract
1 20-ounce can crushed pineapple in heavy syrup, undrained
1 18-ounce box yellow cake mix
1½ cups chopped toasted pecans
½ cup butter, melted

Preheat oven to 350°.
In a saucepan, mix sugar, cornstarch and 1 cup blueberries, mashed. Cook and stir over medium heat until clear and thickened, about 4 minutes. Stir in remaining blueberries and lemon juice; cook 1 minute. Stir in vanilla. Spoon blueberry mixture into a 13x9-inch glass baking dish. Layer with pineapple. Sprinkle cake mix evenly over top. Sprinkle evenly with chopped pecans. Pour butter evenly over all. Do not stir. Bake about 1 hour.

*If using the 21-ounce can pie filling, skip the sugar and cornstarch. Start by stirring lemon juice and vanilla into the blueberry filling and spooning filling into baking dish, then layer with pineapple; top with cake mix; sprinkle with pecans; drizzle with butter. Bake as above.

Makes 12 servings.

BLUEBERRY-CRANBERRY-RAISIN FRUITCAKE

Bake this cake ahead of time for the holidays.

2 cups walnut halves, toasted, chopped
1¼ cups golden raisins
1 cup dried blueberries
1 cup dried cranberries
2 tablespoons all-purpose flour
1½ cups granulated sugar
1 cup butter, softened
5 large eggs
½ cup brandy
1 tablespoon pure vanilla extract
2 cups all-purpose flour, mixed with 2 teaspoons baking powder
and 1 teaspoon salt
⅔ cup walnut halves, toasted
½ cup apple jelly, melted

Preheat oven to 325°.
Mix chopped walnuts, raisins, blueberries, cranberries and flour; set aside.
Beat sugar and butter on low speed until blended; beat 2 minutes on high
speed or until creamy. Beat in eggs, brandy, vanilla. Gradually beat in flour
mixture on low speed. By hand, stir in chopped walnut-fruit mixture.

Spoon batter into a greased 9-inch tube pan with removable bottom. Top
with walnut halves. Bake about 1 hour and 15 minutes or until a wooden
pick inserted in center comes out clean. Cool 10 minutes in pan on a wire
rack. Loosen cake from sides. Invert cake on a plate; remove side and
bottom of pan from cake; invert cake on a wire rack; cool completely. Wrap
in plastic food wrap and store in refrigerator. Brush cake with melted jelly
just before serving. Refrigerate leftovers.

Makes 24 servings.

BLUEBERRY-FILLED LAYER CAKE

Blueberry filling in an orange-flavored cream cheese frosted cake!

Cake
½ cup plus 2 tablespoons soft butter
1½ cups granulated sugar
3 tablespoons frozen orange juice concentrate, thawed
1½ teaspoons freshly grated orange peel
1 teaspoon pure vanilla extract
4 large eggs
2½ cups cake flour
2 teaspoons baking powder
½ teaspoon salt
1 cup whole milk

Filling
4 cups fresh blueberries
2 tablespoons granulated sugar
1 teaspoon fresh lemon juice

Frosting
1 8-ounce package cream cheese
½ cup butter
3¼ cups powdered sugar
2 tablespoons frozen orange juice
    concentrate, thawed
1 teaspoon grated orange peel
½ teaspoon pure vanilla extract

Preheat oven to 350°.
Beat butter and sugar until light and fluffy. Beat in next three ingredients; beat in eggs one at a time. Mix flour, baking powder and salt; beat in creamed mixture alternately with milk. Pour batter into two 9-inch buttered and floured round cake pans. Bake about 30 minutes or until a wooden pick inserted in center comes out clean. Cool in pans on rack.

In a saucepan, mix all filling ingredients; mash berries; cook 8 minutes. Cool. Place 1 cake layer flat side up on a plate. Spread with filling. Chill. Top with second layer flat side down. Beat all frosting ingredients. Frost all over with cream cheese frosting. Refrigerate. Serve at room temperature.

Makes 12 servings.

BLUEBERRY FUNNY CAKE

Not worth the effort

This funny blueberry cake, baked in a pie crust, is adapted from a Palmetto, Louisiana, recipe.

2 cups fresh blueberries
½ cup granulated sugar
2 tablespoons fresh lemon juice
¼ cup butter, room temperature
¼ cup granulated sugar
1 egg
1 teaspoon pure vanilla extract
1¼ cups all-purpose flour
1 teaspoon baking powder
½ teaspoon salt
½ cup milk
1 unbaked 9-inch pie crust

Preheat oven to 375°.
In a saucepan, stir blueberries, ½ cup sugar and lemon juice over medium heat; bring to a simmer, stirring gently until sugar is dissolved. Cool.

Beat butter and ¼ cup sugar with an electric mixer until light and fluffy. Beat in egg and vanilla.

Mix flour, baking powder and salt; stir into butter mixture alternately with milk. Fold in cooled blueberry mixture. Pour batter into unbaked pie crust. Bake about 30–35 minutes or until a wooden pick inserted in center comes out clean.

Makes 8 servings.

BLUEBERRY OATMEAL BREAKFAST CAKE

Good anytime...best served warm.

Cake
1⅓ cups all-purpose flour
¾ cup quick-cooking oatmeal, uncooked
⅓ cup granulated sugar
2 teaspoons baking powder
¼ teaspoon salt
1 teaspoon pure vanilla extract
1 large egg, beaten
¾ cup whole milk
¼ cup corn oil or melted margarine
1 cup frozen blueberries

Icing
1 cup powdered sugar
1 tablespoon milk, about
½ teaspoon pure vanilla extract

Preheat oven to 400°.
Mix flour, oatmeal, granulated sugar, baking powder and salt. In another bowl, mix vanilla, egg, milk and corn oil. Add to dry mixture. Stir until just moistened. Fold in blueberries. Spoon batter into a greased 8-inch round cake pan. Bake 20–25 minutes or until a wooden pick inserted in center comes out clean.

Mix all icing ingredients. Drizzle over cake.

Makes 8 servings.

BLUEBERRY PUNCH BOWL CAKE

A cake mix is used in this recipe...easy and good.

1 18-ounce package butter cake mix with pudding
1 5-ounce package vanilla flavor instant pudding and pie filling
2 21-ounce cans blueberry pie filling, divided
1 20-ounce can crushed pineapple, undrained, divided
1 12-ounce container frozen whipped topping, thawed, divided
½ cup chopped nuts, divided

Prepare cake mix according to package directions for a 13x9-inch pan; cool. Prepare pudding mix according to package directions; set aside.

Crumble half of cooled cake onto bottom of a large glass bowl (punch bowl). Layer with half of pudding, half of pineapple, 1 can blueberry pie filling, half of whipped topping and half of chopped nuts. Repeat. Store in refrigerator.

Makes 15 servings.

BLUEBERRY SOUR CREAM CAKE

Serve warm or cold.

2 cups all-purpose flour
1 teaspoon baking soda
1 teaspoon baking powder
½ teaspoon salt
½ cup butter
1 cup granulated sugar
3 eggs
2 teaspoons pure vanilla extract
1 16-ounce container dairy sour cream
2 cups blueberries, divided
½ cup brown sugar

Preheat oven to 350°.
Mix flour, soda, baking powder and salt; set aside.

Beat butter and sugar until light and fluffy. Beat in eggs, one at a time. Add vanilla. Stir in flour mixture alternately with sour cream. Fold in 1 cup blueberries. Pour half of batter into a greased and floured 13x9-inch baking pan. Sprinkle with 1 cup blueberries; sprinkle with brown sugar. Pour remaining batter over top. Bake about 45–50 minutes or until a wooden pick inserted in center comes out clean. Serve with whipped cream. Store in refrigerator.

Makes 12 servings.

BLUEBERRY UPSIDE-DOWN CAKE

Not just for pineapple anymore...serve this cake warm.

2 cups fresh blueberries
½ cup granulated sugar
2 tablespoons all-purpose flour
3 tablespoons freshly grated lemon rind
½ cup butter, softened
1 cup granulated sugar
3 eggs
1 teaspoon pure vanilla extract
¼ teaspoon almond extract
¾ cup whole milk
2 cups all-purpose flour
4 teaspoons baking powder
¼ teaspoon salt
½ cup toasted slivered almonds
sweetened whipped cream

Preheat oven to 350°.
Mix blueberries, ½ cup sugar, 2 tablespoons flour and lemon rind; spread evenly into a greased and floured 9-inch springform pan.

Beat butter and 1 cup sugar until fluffy; beat in eggs and extracts. Mix flour, baking powder and salt; beat into creamy mixture alternately with milk until just moistened. Pour over blueberries. Bake 60–70 minutes or until a wooden pick inserted in center comes out clean.

Place a serving plate over top of pan; carefully invert cake and plate together. Remove sides from cake pan. Serve warm, topped with almonds. Garnish with sweetened whipped cream as desired. Refrigerate leftovers.

Makes 12 servings.

CHOCOLATE-FROSTED LEMON-BLUEBERRY CAKE

White chocolate and cream cheese frosted cake.

Cake
- ¾ cup butter
- 2 cups granulated sugar
- ⅓ cup fresh lemon juice, mixed with 1 teaspoon grated lemon peel
- 1 teaspoon pure vanilla extract
- 4 large eggs
- 3¼ cups cake flour
- ½ teaspoon each—salt, baking powder, baking soda
- 1 cup buttermilk
- 2½ cups fresh blueberries

Frosting
- 2 6-ounce packages white baking chocolate with cocoa butter, finely chopped
- 11 ounces cream cheese, softened
- ¾ cup butter, softened
- 1½ tablespoons fresh lemon juice

Preheat oven to 350°.
Beat butter and sugar until fluffy. Beat in lemon juice, vanilla and eggs.

Mix dry ingredients; beat into creamed mixture, alternating with buttermilk; fold in blueberries; pour batter into two 9-inch round parchment-lined, cake baking pans. Bake 40 minutes or until a wooden pick inserted in center comes out clean. Cool in pan. Remove parchment; place first layer, flat side up on a plate; spread with 1 cup frosting (see directions below). Top with second layer, flat side down; frost top and sides. Store in refrigerator.

Melt chocolate, stirring until smooth; cool to lukewarm. In a large bowl, beat cream cheese and butter; beat in lemon juice and cooled chocolate.

Makes 12 servings.

CREAM AND BLUEBERRY CUPCAKES

These little cakes are split and filled.

2⅔ cups cake flour
1 tablespoon baking powder
¾ teaspoon salt
1⅔ cups granulated sugar
¾ cup butter or margarine, softened
3 large eggs
1½ teaspoons pure vanilla extract
1 cup whole milk
1 cup heavy whipping cream, whipped with 2 tablespoons
   granulated sugar and ½ teaspoon pure vanilla extract
4 cups fresh blueberries

Preheat oven to 375°.
Mix flour, baking powder and salt; set aside.

Beat sugar and butter on high speed until light and fluffy. Beat in eggs one
at a time. Add vanilla. Using low speed, add flour mixture and milk alternately, beginning and ending with flour.

Fill paper-lined muffin cups ⅔ full. Bake about 20 minutes or until a wooden
pick inserted in center comes out clean. Remove from oven. Cool in pan.

Remove paper liners. Split cakes in half horizontally. Spread bottom half
with whipped cream mixture and blueberries; replace top half and repeat.

Makes 24 cupcakes.

CREAMY BLUEBERRY CAKE

For best flavor, serve a day after preparing...if you can wait!

Cake
1 18-ounce package yellow cake mix

Filling
1 21-ounce can blueberry pie filling

Frosting
½ cup granulated sugar
½ cup powdered sugar
1 3-ounce package cream cheese, softened
1 teaspoon pure vanilla extract
1 12-ounce container non-dairy whipped topping, thawed

Prepare cake mix according to package directions for two 9-inch round cake pans. Cool completely.

Cut each cake layer in half horizontally, using a serrated knife. Place one layer on a serving plate. Top with ⅓ of the blueberry pie filling. Repeat layering, ending with cake layer. Frost sides and top with cream cheese frosting (see directions below). Store in refrigerator.

In a bowl, beat sugars, cream cheese and vanilla until smooth. Fold in whipped topping. Store in refrigerator.

Makes 12 servings.

CREAMY CHEESE-FROSTED BLUEBERRY LEMON CAKE

A lemon cake mix is used for this delicious cake.

Cake
1 18-ounce package lemon cake mix
½ cup fresh orange juice
½ cup water
⅓ cup corn oil
3 eggs
1½ cups blueberries
2 teaspoons freshly grated orange peel

Filling/Frosting
1 3-ounce package cream cheese, softened
¼ cup butter, softened
3 cups powdered sugar
2 tablespoons fresh orange juice, mixed with ½ teaspoon pure vanilla extract
1 cup whipping cream, whipped with 2 tablespoons powdered sugar

Preheat oven to 325°.
Beat cake mix, orange juice, water, corn oil and eggs on low speed for 30 seconds; beat on medium speed 2 minutes. Fold in blueberries and orange peel. Pour batter into two greased and floured 8-inch round cake pans. Bake 35–40 minutes or until a wooden pick inserted in center comes out clean. Cool in pans on a rack 10 minutes; remove from pans and cool completely on a wire rack.

In a bowl, beat cream cheese and butter until fluffy; beat in sugar, orange juice and vanilla. Fold in whipped cream; fill and frost cake with mixture. Store in refrigerator.

Makes 12 servings.

FAVORITE BLUEBERRY POUND CAKE

Butter is better...but margarine will do too.

2 cups granulated sugar
1 cup butter, softened
1 tablespoon pure vanilla extract
4 eggs
3 cups all-purpose flour, divided
½ teaspoon baking powder
2 cups fresh or frozen blueberries, thaw if frozen
1 cup coarsely chopped pecans

Preheat oven to 325°.
In a large mixer bowl, beat sugar and butter until light and fluffy. Add vanilla. Beat in eggs, one at a time until well blended.

Mix 2 cups flour and baking powder; gradually beat into creamed mixture until smooth.

Mix blueberries, pecans and remaining flour until coated. Carefully fold into batter. Sprinkle 1 tablespoon granulated sugar into bottom of a greased 10-inch tube pan, then pour in batter. Bake 1 hour and 15 minutes or until a wooden pick inserted in center comes out clean. Cool in pan 10 minutes. Invert on cooling rack; cool completely. Sprinkle with powdered sugar when serving.

Makes 16 servings.

FULL OF BLUEBERRIES CAKE

This one is full of the good berries.

½ cup butter, softened
⅓ cup granulated sugar
1 whole egg
2 teaspoons pure vanilla extract
1½ cups all-purpose flour
1½ teaspoons baking powder
¼ teaspoon salt
4 cups fresh blueberries
⅓ cup granulated sugar
1 teaspoon pure vanilla extract
2 cups dairy sour cream
2 egg yolks, slightly beaten
¼ teaspoon ground cardamom or ground nutmeg
¼ teaspoon freshly grated lemon rind

Preheat oven to 350°.
On low speed, beat butter and ⅓ cup sugar until light and fluffy. Beat in whole egg and 2 teaspoons vanilla.

Mix flour, baking powder and salt; gradually stir into creamy mixture until well blended. Spread mixture onto bottom of a greased 9-inch springform pan. Top with blueberries.

Mix ⅓ cup sugar, 1 teaspoon vanilla, sour cream, egg yolks, cardamom and lemon rind; pour over blueberries. Bake 50–55 minutes or until set; do not overbake. Loosen collar, but cool completely before removing sides from pan. Store in refrigerator.

Makes 10 servings.

NO-BAKE FRUITCAKE
WITH DRIED BLUEBERRIES

Candied fruit, pecans, blueberries, graham cracker crumbs and spice!

2 cups miniature marshmallows
⅔ cup evaporated milk
6 tablespoons orange juice
1 teaspoon pure vanilla extract
1 cup chopped pecans
1 cup candied mixed fruit
¾ cup diced dates
¾ cup raisins
⅓ cup dried blueberries
¼ cup candied cherries
4 cups graham cracker crumbs
1 teaspoon ground cinnamon
1 teaspoon ground nutmeg
½ teaspoon ground cloves

In a 3-quart saucepan, heat marshmallows, evaporated milk and orange juice until marshmallows are completely melted. Stir in vanilla.

Mix remaining ingredients. Add first mixture. Press mixture firmly into a 6-cup ring mold or a loaf pan lined with waxed paper. Cover tightly with plastic food wrap. Refrigerate and chill at least 2 days before serving.

Makes 1 fruitcake.

PUMPKIN-BLUEBERRY CAKE

The great pumpkin and dried blueberries...a great cake!

Cake
2 cups each, all-purpose flour, granulated sugar
2 teaspoons baking powder
1 teaspoon each—baking soda, ground cinnamon, ground nutmeg
¼ teaspoon ground cloves
½ teaspoon salt
1 cup corn oil
4 eggs
1 15-ounce can pumpkin puree
½ cup chopped nuts
⅓ cup dried blueberries
⅓ cup raisins

Frosting
⅓ cup butter, softened
1 3-ounce package cream cheese, softened
2 cups powdered sugar
1 tablespoon orange juice, about
1 teaspoon pure vanilla extract

Preheat oven to 350°.
Mix all cake ingredients except nuts, blueberries and raisins. Beat on low speed until moistened, then 2 minutes on medium speed. Stir in nuts, blueberries and raisins. Pour into a greased 13x9-inch pan. Bake 40–50 minutes or until a wooden pick comes out clean. Cool in pan completely, then frost. Store in refrigerator.

Beat all frosting ingredients until smooth.

Makes 12 servings.

RASPBERRY-BLUEBERRY PUDDING CAKE

Serve this pudding cake with vanilla ice cream or frozen yogurt.

1½ **cups blueberries, fresh or frozen, thawed**
1½ **cups raspberries, fresh or frozen, thawed**
1 **cup all-purpose flour**
1 **teaspoon baking powder**
¼ **teaspoon salt**
¾ **cup granulated sugar**
½ **cup whole milk**
3 **tablespoons butter, melted**
1 **teaspoon pure vanilla extract**
¾ **cup granulated sugar**
1 **tablespoon cornstarch**
1 **cup boiling water**

Preheat oven to 350°.
Spread berries evenly into a buttered 9-inch square baking pan.

Mix flour, baking powder, salt and ¾ cups sugar. Add milk, butter and vanilla. Beat until smooth; spread batter over berries.

Mix ¾ cup sugar and cornstarch; sprinkle evenly over batter. Pour boiling water on top. Bake 45 minutes or until a wooden pick inserted in center comes out clean.

Makes 8 servings.

ALMOND-TOPPED BLUEBERRY COFFEE CAKE

Make this coffee cake a day ahead of time...easy to reheat for that morning coffee break.

2 cups all-purpose flour
2 teaspoons baking powder
¾ teaspoon salt
½ cup butter, softened
1¼ cups granulated sugar
2 large eggs
1 teaspoon pure vanilla extract
½ cup whole milk
2 cups blueberries
1 egg white
3 tablespoons granulated sugar
1 cup sliced almonds

Preheat oven to 350°.
Mix flour, baking powder and salt; set aside. Beat butter and 1¼ cups sugar until fluffy. Beat in 2 eggs and vanilla. Add flour mixture and milk alternately, beating on low speed until just moistened. Fold in blueberries. Spoon batter into a buttered 2½-quart glass baking dish.

In a small bowl, beat egg white lightly. Stir in 3 tablespoons granulated sugar and almonds. Spoon mixture over batter. Bake 50–60 minutes or until a wooden pick inserted in center comes out clean. Serve warm.

Makes 8 servings.

CREAM CHEESE BLUEBERRY COFFEE CAKE

Blueberry preserves and cream cheese in this coffee cake.

1¾ cups all-purpose flour
½ cup granulated sugar
¾ cup butter, softened
2 eggs
½ teaspoon baking powder
½ teaspoon baking soda
¼ teaspoon salt
1 teaspoon pure vanilla extract

Topping
¼ cup granulated sugar
1 8-ounce package cream cheese, softened
1 large egg
1 teaspoon grated lemon peel
1 10-ounce jar blueberry preserves
½ cup powdered sugar, mixed with 2 teaspoons fresh lemon juice

Preheat oven to 350°.
Beat first eight ingredients on low speed. Beat 2 minutes on medium speed. Spread batter on bottom and 2 inches up sides of a greased and floured springform pan.

Beat all topping ingredients except preserves and powdered sugar mixture; pour over batter. Top evenly with preserves. Bake 45–55 minutes. Cool 20 minutes. Remove sides from pan. Drizzle top with powdered sugar mixture. Serve warm or cold. Store in refrigerator.

Makes 16 servings.

FRESH BLUEBERRIES 'N' CREAM CHEESE COFFEE CAKE

A good coffee cake to serve for that special coffee.

1¼ cups granulated sugar
½ cup butter
2 eggs, slightly beaten
2 cups all-purpose flour
1 tablespoon baking powder
1 teaspoon salt
¾ cup whole milk
¼ cup water
1 teaspoon pure vanilla extract
2 cups fresh blueberries, mixed with ¼ cup all-purpose flour
1 8-ounce package cream cheese, cubed
1 teaspoon freshly grated lemon rind

Topping
¼ cup each—all-purpose flour, granulated sugar
1 teaspoon freshly grated lemon rind
2 tablespoons butter

Preheat oven to 375°.
In a bowl, beat sugar with butter until light and fluffy. Stir in eggs. Mix flour, baking powder and salt. Add alternately to creamed mixture with milk and water until well mixed. Stir in vanilla. Fold in blueberries, cream cheese and lemon rind. Pour mixture into a greased and floured 13x9-inch baking pan.

Mix all topping ingredients until mixture resembles coarse crumbs. Sprinkle over batter. Bake 1 hour. Store in refrigerator.

Makes 16 servings.

LOUISIANA BLUEBERRY STREUSEL COFFEE CAKE

Sour cream, pecans and blueberries...a wonderful coffee cake.

¾ **cup granulated sugar**
½ **cup butter**
3 eggs
1 teaspoon pure vanilla extract
2 cups all-purpose flour mixed with 1½ teaspoons baking powder
1 8-ounce container dairy sour cream, mixed with 1 teaspoon baking soda
2 cups fresh or frozen blueberries

Topping
1½ cups brown sugar, packed
4 teaspoons ground cinnamon
1 cup chopped pecans

Preheat oven to 350°.
Beat granulated sugar and butter until light and fluffy. Beat in eggs and vanilla. Gradually beat in flour mixture, on low speed, until well mixed. Stir in sour cream mixture; mix well. Spread half the batter into a greased 13x9-inch pan. Sprinkle evenly with all the blueberries.

Mix brown sugar, cinnamon and pecans; sprinkle half evenly over blueberries. Spoon dollops of remaining batter evenly over all and then spread carefully. Sprinkle evenly with remaining topping mixture. Bake about 40–50 minutes or until a wooden pick inserted in center comes out clean. Best served warm.

Makes 16 servings.

MINNESOTA BLUEBERRY COFFEE CAKE

Blueberry pie filling is used in this good coffee cake.

1 cup granulated sugar
½ cup butter, softened
1 cup dairy sour cream
2 eggs
1 teaspoon pure vanilla extract
2 cups all-purpose flour
1½ teaspoons baking powder
½ teaspoon baking soda
½ teaspoon salt
1 21-ounce can blueberry pie filling

Topping
¼ cup all-purpose flour
¼ cup granulated sugar
¼ cup chopped pecans
1 teaspoon ground cinnamon
3 tablespoons butter

Preheat oven to 325°.
Beat sugar and softened butter until creamy. Add sour cream, eggs and vanilla; beat until well blended. Add flour, baking powder, baking soda and salt; beat on low speed until well blended. Spoon half the batter into a greased and floured 13x9-inch pan. Top evenly with blueberry pie filling. Spread evenly with remaining batter.

Mix all topping ingredients until crumbly. Sprinkle over batter. Bake 45–50 minutes.

Makes 16 servings.

PLAIN BLUEBERRY COFFEE CAKE

Not fancy, but very good when freshly baked. Will freeze well.

½ cup whole milk
½ cup margarine, melted
2 eggs, beaten
1 teaspoon pure vanilla extract
2 cups fresh blueberries
2 cups all-purpose flour
1 cup granulated sugar
2 teaspoons baking powder
½ teaspoon salt

Topping
½ cup all-purpose flour
½ cup granulated sugar
¼ cup butter, softened
1 teaspoon ground cinnamon

Preheat oven to 350°.
Mix milk, margarine, eggs and vanilla. Mix flour, sugar, baking powder and salt until well blended; add to first mixture. Fold in blueberries. Pour batter into an 8x10-inch or similar size baking pan.

Mix all topping ingredients until crumbly. Sprinkle evenly over batter. Bake 45–50 minutes or until a wooden pick inserted in center comes out clean.

Makes 10 servings.

BLUEBERRY-PEACH SHORTCAKE

A purchased sponge cake is used for this easy dessert.

1 8-ounce package cream cheese, softened
1 14-ounce can sweetened condensed milk
⅓ cup lemon juice
1 teaspoon pure vanilla extract
1 6-ounce prepared sponge cake
2 tablespoons granulated sugar
2 teaspoons cornstarch
¼ cup water, mixed with 1 teaspoon lemon juice
1 cup fresh blueberries
3 ripe medium-size peaches, peeled and sliced

Beat cream cheese until fluffy. Gradually beat in sweetened condensed milk until smooth. Stir in lemon juice and vanilla; spread on top of cake; chill.

In a saucepan, mix sugar and cornstarch. Stir in water and lemon juice mixture; cook and stir until thickened. Add blueberries; cook until bubbly. Chill.

To serve, arrange peaches on top of cake; top with chilled blueberry sauce. Refrigerate any leftovers.

Makes 8 servings.

BLUEBERRY-STRAWBERRY SHORTCAKE

An all-time favorite.

Shortcake Biscuits
2 cups all-purpose flour
¼ cup granulated sugar
2 teaspoons baking powder
1 teaspoon salt
⅓ cup cold butter
¾ cup whole milk
1½ teaspoons granulated sugar, mixed with ⅛ teaspoon
  ground cinnamon

Filling
1 cup fresh blueberries
1 cup fresh strawberries, sliced
1 tablespoon granulated sugar
1 cup whipping cream, whipped with 1 tablespoon granulated
  sugar and 1 teaspoon pure vanilla extract

Preheat oven to 450°.
Mix flour, sugar, baking powder and salt. Cut in butter with a pastry blender until crumbly. Stir in milk with a fork to moisten; form a ball. Knead on a floured surface until dough is smooth. Roll out to a 9x6-inch rectangle, ½ inch thick. Cut out 6 rounds with a 3-inch biscuit cutter. Place on an ungreased baking sheet. Sprinkle with sugar-cinnamon mixture. Bake until lightly browned, about 12 minutes. Remove from baking sheet; cool slightly, then split in half horizontally.

For filling, mix berries and 1 tablespoon sugar. When serving, top bottom half with 2 tablespoons whipped cream and ⅓ cup berries. Top with other half of shortcake. Top with more whipped cream.

Makes 6 servings.

FRESH PEACH-BLUEBERRY SHORTCAKE

Cardamom-flavored biscuits with creamy fruit filling.

Shortcake Biscuits
3 cups all-purpose flour
½ cup light brown sugar, packed
4 teaspoons baking powder
¾ teaspoon baking soda
1½ teaspoons ground cardamom
½ teaspoon salt
¾ cup cold butter, cut up
3 eggs, beaten
½ cup buttermilk, mixed with
   1½ teaspoons pure vanilla extract
melted butter
granulated sugar

Filling
8 ripe peaches, peeled,
   pitted and sliced
4 cups fresh blueberries
¾ cup granulated sugar
2 teaspoons pure vanilla extract
½ teaspoon ground cardamom
⅔ cup dairy sour cream
1 cup whipping cream,
   whipped with 1 tablespoon
   powdered sugar

Preheat oven to 425°.
Mix first six ingredients. Cut in butter with a pastry blender until mixture resembles coarse meal. Stir in eggs, buttermilk-vanilla with a fork to form a dough; knead on a floured surface until smooth. Divide into 3 equal portions; roll each to a 1-inch thick round; cut into 4 wedges. Place on a baking sheet. Brush with melted butter and sprinkle tops with granulated sugar. Bake about 15 minutes. Cool on a rack.

Mix peaches, blueberries, sugar, vanilla and cardamom. In another bowl, mix sour cream and whipped cream.

Split warm biscuits in half horizontally. To serve, place bottom halves in individual bowls; spoon fruit over biscuits. Top with some of the cream mixture. Replace top halves; cover with more cream mixture. Refrigerate leftovers immediately.

Makes 12 servings.

BLUEBERRY CHEESECAKE CUPCAKES

A nice treat for an afternoon tea.

1 dozen sugar cookies
1 8-ounce package cream cheese, softened
¾ cup granulated sugar
2 eggs
½ cup dairy sour cream
1 teaspoon pure vanilla extract
½ teaspoon freshly grated lemon rind
3 tablespoons all-purpose flour
1 cup blueberries
sweetened whipped cream

Preheat oven to 325°.
Line muffin cups with foil baking liners. Place a cookie into bottom of each liner, trimming to fit if needed.

Beat cream cheese and sugar on medium speed until smooth. Beat in eggs just until blended. Beat in sour cream, vanilla and lemon rind. Gradually beat in flour on low speed. By hand, stir in blueberries. Spoon mixture equally over each cookie. Bake 30–35 minutes or until set. Remove from oven; cool in pan 10 minutes. Remove from pan; cool on a rack. Refrigerate immediately. When serving, top with sweetened whipped cream.

Makes 12 servings.

BLUEBERRY-STRAWBERRY
HOT FUDGE CHEESECAKE

Pure pleasure.

Crust
1½ cups graham cracker crumbs
¼ cup granulated sugar
⅓ cup butter, melted
¾ cup hot fudge sauce, heated just before spreading on crust

4 8-ounce packages cream cheese, softened
1⅓ cups granulated sugar
1¼ teaspoons pure vanilla extract
4 eggs
⅓ cup blueberry preserves, melted
¼ cup strawberry preserves, melted
fresh blueberries and fresh sliced strawberries

Preheat oven to 325°.
Mix all crust ingredients except hot fudge sauce; press onto bottom and 2
inches up sides of a 9-inch springform pan with 3-inch sides. Bake 5 minutes. Remove from oven. Pour heated hot fudge sauce over crust.

Beat cream cheese until smooth. Gradually beat in sugar and vanilla. Beat
in eggs, one at a time. Pour over hot fudge sauce. Bake 55–65 minutes or
until set. Cool 15 minutes, then run a metal spatula along side of cake to
loosen. Cover and refrigerate 8 hours. Spread melted blueberry preserves
over cheesecake, then make a zig-zag pattern on top with melted strawberry preserves. Top with fresh berries. Remove pan sides just before
serving. Refrigerate leftovers immediately.

Makes 16 servings.

BLUEBERRY MINI-CHEESECAKES

Recipe adapted from my cookbook, *I Love Cheesecake*.

Crust
20 vanilla wafers

Filling
2 8-ounce packages cream cheese, softened
½ cup granulated sugar
1 teaspoon pure vanilla extract
½ teaspoon freshly grated lemon rind
2 eggs

Topping
1 21-ounce can blueberry pie filling
sweetened whipped cream
fresh blueberries

Preheat oven to 325°.
Place paper liners in muffin cups. Place 1 vanilla wafer in each.

Beat cream cheese and sugar until fluffy. Add vanilla and lemon rind. Beat in eggs, one at a time. Spoon mixture equally over wafers. Bake about 20 minutes or until set. Cool in pan on a wire rack.

Top with blueberry pie filling as desired; chill well. Top with sweetened whipped cream, and garnish with fresh blueberries as desired. Store in refrigerator.

Makes 20 servings.

CRANBERRY-BLUEBERRY-TOPPED SPICE CHEESECAKE

Cranberry sauce, dried blueberries and spice cake mix...good.

Crust
1 18-ounce box moist spice cake mix
½ cup butter, melted
1 egg

Filling
2 8-ounce packages cream cheese, softened
1 14-ounce can sweetened condensed milk (not evaporated)
¼ cup fresh lemon juice
1 teaspoon pure vanilla extract
2 tablespoons cornstarch, mixed with 1 tablespoon brown sugar
1 16-ounce can whole berry cranberry sauce mixed with ⅓ cup
 dried blueberries

Topping
1 cup reserved cake mixture
¾ cup chopped walnuts
½ cup quick-cooking oatmeal,
 uncooked

Preheat oven to 350°.
Mix cake mix, butter and egg until well blended; reserve 1 cup mixture for topping. Press remaining mixture onto bottom of a 10-inch springform pan.

Beat cream cheese until smooth; beat in condensed milk, lemon juice, vanilla and cornstarch mixture; spoon over prepared crust. Spoon cranberry mixture over cheese layer.

Mix all topping ingredients and sprinkle evenly over cake. Bake 40–45 minutes or until set. Cool completely on a wire rack. Chill at least 2 hours before serving. Refrigerate.

Makes 16 servings.

HANNAH'S BLUEBERRY-TOPPED CHEESECAKE

This recipe is adapted from my book, *I Love Cheesecake*.

Crust
1¼ cups graham cracker crumbs
¼ cup granulated sugar
¼ cup butter, melted

Filling
1 8-ounce package cream cheese, softened
½ cup granulated sugar
½ cup dairy sour cream
2 eggs, beaten
1 teaspoon pure vanilla extract

Topping
¼ cup granulated sugar, mixed with 1½ tablespoons cornstarch
¼ teaspoon each—salt, ground cinnamon
½ cup water, mixed with 2 teaspoons fresh lemon juice
2 cups blueberries
½ teaspoon pure vanilla extract
sweetened whipped cream

Preheat oven to 350°.
Mix all crust ingredients. Press mixture onto bottom and a little up sides of an 8-inch square baking pan; set aside.

Beat all filling ingredients until creamy. Pour into prepared crust. Bake 20–25 minutes or until set. Cool on a rack. Chill.

In a saucepan, stir sugar, cornstarch, salt, cinnamon and water until thickened. Stir in blueberries; stir and cook 3 minutes or a little longer if using frozen berries. Stir in vanilla. Cool. Spread over cheesecake when serving and top with whipped cream. Store in refrigerator.

Makes 8 servings.

RED, WHITE AND BLUE CHEESECAKE

Make this one for the 4th of July...or any festive day!

Crust
1½ cups graham cracker crumbs
¼ cup granulated sugar
5 tablespoons butter, melted

Filling
1 21-ounce can blueberry pie filling
3 8-ounce packages cream cheese, softened
¾ cup granulated sugar
1 teaspoon pure vanilla extract
4 eggs

Topping
sweetened whipped cream
fresh sliced strawberries
fresh blueberries

Preheat oven to 325°.
Mix all crust ingredients. Press onto bottom of a 13x9-inch pan. Bake 6 minutes. Remove from oven. Cool.

Spoon blueberry filling into crust. Beat cream cheese until fluffy. Beat in sugar and vanilla. Beat in eggs, one at a time. Carefully pour mixture over blueberries; smooth gently. Bake 45–50 minutes or until just set. Chill well. Store in refrigerator. When serving, top with whipped cream, and garnish with strawberries and blueberries.

Makes 16 servings.

THE GIRLS' QUICK
BLUEBERRY CHEESECAKE

The girls all "purr" for this delicious cheesecake.

Crust
1 18-ounce package moist yellow cake mix
⅓ cup butter, softened
1 large egg

Filling
3 8-ounce packages cream cheese, softened
¾ cup granulated sugar
3 eggs
1 cup dairy sour cream
2 teaspoons pure vanilla extract

Topping
1 21-ounce can blueberry pie filling
sweetened whipped cream

Preheat oven to 350°.
Mix all crust ingredients on low speed until crumbly. Press onto bottom of a greased and floured 13x9-inch pan. Bake 18 minutes. Reduce heat to 300°.

Beat cream cheese until light. Add remaining filling ingredients; beat until smooth. Pour into prepared crust. Bake 45–55 minutes or until center is set. Cool, then refrigerate. Chill well. When serving, top with blueberry filling. Garnish with whipped cream as desired. Store leftovers in refrigerator.

Makes 15 servings.

Pies
Tarts
Tortes
Pastries

ALMOND-CRUSTED BLUEBERRY ICE CREAM PIE

An easy pie to prepare days ahead of time needed.

Crust
2½ cups slivered almonds, blanched, toasted and finely chopped
¼ cup brown sugar, packed
1 tablespoon granulated sugar
¼ teaspoon ground cinnamon
5 tablespoons butter, melted

Filling
2 pints blueberry ice cream or vanilla ice cream

Topping
½ cup whipping cream
1 tablespoon granulated sugar
½ teaspoon pure vanilla extract
⅛ teaspoon ground cinnamon
2 cups fresh blueberries

Preheat oven to 350°.
Mix all crust ingredients in a 10-inch glass pie plate. Press onto bottom and up sides. Bake until lightly golden, about 10 minutes. Remove from oven; cool completely.

Soften ice cream, but do not melt. Spoon into crust. Freeze. Whip cream, granulated sugar, vanilla and cinnamon to stiff peaks; spread over pie when serving. Top with blueberries. Freeze leftovers.

Makes 8 servings.

APPLE-BLUEBERRY-CRANBERRY PIE

Fresh apples, fresh blueberries and dried cranberries...a holiday treat.

Crust
2 cups all-purpose flour
¼ teaspoon salt
⅓ cup cold butter
⅓ cup solid vegetable shortening
5–7 tablespoons cold water

Filling
8 tart baking apples, peeled,
**   cored and thinly sliced**
¾ cup granulated sugar
¼ cup all-purpose flour, mixed
**   with ½ teaspoon ground cinnamon**
1 teaspoon freshly grated lemon
**   rind, mixed with 2 teaspoons**
**   lemon juice**
1 teaspoon pure vanilla extract
2 cups fresh blueberries
½ cup dried cranberries
3 tablespoons butter, cut up

Preheat oven to 400°.
Mix flour and salt; cut in butter and shortening until mixture resembles coarse meal. Stir in enough water with a fork until moistened. Divide dough in half. Roll each half out on a floured surface to a 12-inch circle. Place one into a 9-inch pie pan. Trim, leaving a 1-inch overhang.

Mix apples, sugar, flour, lemon rind, juice and vanilla; spoon half the mixture into crust; sprinkle with half the blueberries and half the cranberries. Repeat. Dot with butter. Top with second crust; seal and flute. Cut several slits on top to vent. Place on a baking sheet. Bake 20 minutes. Reduce heat to 375° and bake until apples are done, about 40 minutes. Cool one hour before serving with vanilla ice cream. Refrigerate leftovers.

Makes 8 servings.

7.5.07
V. good!

BLUEBERRY CUSTARD CREAM PIE

Almost like a banana cream pie...you could add bananas if inclined.

Crust
1¾-2
- 1⅓ cups vanilla wafer crumbs
- 2 tablespoons granulated sugar
- *8* ~~5~~ tablespoons butter, melted

Filling
- ½ cup granulated sugar
- ¼ teaspoon salt
- 2 tablespoons all-purpose flour
- 2 tablespoons cornstarch
- 1¾ cups half-and-half (light cream)
- 3 egg yolks, beaten
- 2 tablespoons butter
- 2 teaspoons pure vanilla extract
- *4-* 6 cups fresh blueberries, divided
- ~~⅔ cup granulated sugar~~ *omitted*
- 1 tablespoon cornstarch

Preheat oven to 350°.
Mix all crust ingredients in a 9-inch glass pie plate; press onto bottom and up sides of plate. Bake 8 minutes; cool.

In a saucepan, mix first four filling ingredients. Gradually stir in half-and-half until smooth. Cook, stirring until thickened and boil 2 minutes. Remove from heat; stir some of hot mixture into egg yolks, then stir back into pan; boil 1 minute. Stir in butter and vanilla. Remove from heat; stir in ¾ cup blueberries; pour into crust.

Layer crust w/ banana slices before pouring this in.

1
Crush ~~two~~ cups blueberries in a saucepan; bring to a boil; break up berries. Boil and stir 2 minutes; ~~strain; discard pulp. Add enough water to juice to~~ *Add* ~~measure 1 cup. In the same saucepan, mix sugar and~~ cornstarch. ~~Stir in~~ ~~blueberry juice;~~ boil 2 minutes. Remove from heat; stir in remaining blueberries. Spoon over filling. Chill. Store in refrigerator. *more*

Makes 8 servings.

BLUEBERRY PUDDING PIE

Recipe adapted from my cookbook, *I Love Pies You Don't Bake.*

Crust
1½ cups graham cracker crumbs
¼ cup granulated sugar
⅓ cup butter, melted

Filling
1 8-ounce package cream cheese, softened
1 teaspoon pure vanilla extract
1 14-ounce can sweetened condensed milk
¾ cup cold water
1 3.5-ounce package vanilla flavored instant pudding and pie mix
1 cup whipping cream, whipped
1 21-ounce can blueberry pie filling, chilled

Topping
sweetened whipped cream

Mix all crust ingredients; press onto bottom and sides of a 9-inch pie plate. Chill.

Beat cream cheese until fluffy. Add vanilla. Gradually beat in sweetened condensed milk. On low speed, beat in water and dry pudding mix until smooth. Fold in whipped cream. Pour half the mixture into crust; spread evenly. Top with half the blueberry pie filling. Repeat layers. Refrigerate until set.

Garnish with sweetened whipped cream as desired. Store in refrigerator.

Makes 8 servings.

BLUE-RIBBON BLUEBERRY PIE

A very good pie...serve with vanilla ice cream.

Crust
2 cups all-purpose flour
¼ teaspoon salt
⅓ cup cold butter
⅓ cup cold solid shortening
5–6 tablespoons cold water, about

Filling
½ cup granulated sugar
2 tablespoons all-purpose flour
¼ teaspoon each ground nutmeg and ground cinnamon
¼ teaspoon salt
1 teaspoon pure vanilla extract
6 cups fresh blueberries
1 tablespoon butter, cut up

Preheat oven to 400°.
Mix flour and salt. Cut in butter and shortening with a pastry blender until mixture resembles coarse crumbly meal. Stir in enough water with a fork to just moisten. Divide dough in half and shape each into a ball. Flatten slightly. Roll each on a floured surface to a 12-inch circle. Place one crust into a 9-inch pie pan; press onto bottom and sides. Trim crust, leaving a ½ inch overhang.

Mix sugar, flour, nutmeg, cinnamon and salt. Stir in vanilla and blueberries. Spoon mixture into crust. Dot with butter. Top with second crust. Cut several slits on top to vent. Seal, trim and flute edge. Place on a baking sheet. Bake 55 minutes or until crust is browned and juice is bubbling (cover crust with foil if it's browning too fast). Remove from oven; cool 30 minutes. Serve warm. Refrigerate leftovers.

Makes 8 servings.

COOKIE CRUST BLUEBERRY PIE

Just the crust is baked in this pie.

Crust
1½ cups vanilla wafer crumbs
¼ cup flaked coconut
6 tablespoons butter, melted

Filling
6 cups fresh blueberries, divided
¾ cup granulated sugar
2 tablespoons water
2 tablespoons cornstarch, dissolved in ¼ cup cold water
1 tablespoon butter
2 teaspoons fresh lemon juice
1 teaspoon pure vanilla extract

Preheat oven to 350°.
Mix all crust ingredients in a 9-inch glass pie plate; press firmly onto bottom and up sides. Bake 7 minutes. Cool.

In a saucepan, mix 2 cups blueberries, sugar and water. Bring to a full boil. Stir in cornstarch mixture. Return to a full boil, stirring constantly. Reduce heat to low; cook and stir 2 minutes. Remove from heat; stir in butter, lemon juice, vanilla and remaining blueberries. Pour into crust. Cool to room temperature. Serve with whipped cream. Store in refrigerator.

Makes 8 servings.

FRESH BLUEBERRY-STRAWBERRY MOUSSE PIE

A cool, fresh two-berry pie in a graham cracker crust.

Crust
1¼ cups graham cracker crumbs
2 tablespoons granulated sugar
¼ cup butter, melted

Sauce
2 cups blueberries
¼ cup each—orange juice, water
**¼ cup granulated sugar, mixed
with 1 tablespoon cornstarch**

Filling
1 envelope unflavored gelatin
¼ cup cold water
2 tablespoons fresh lemon juice
1 teaspoon pure vanilla extract
1 cup fresh blueberries, finely chopped
1 cup fresh strawberries, sliced and finely chopped
¾ cup powdered sugar
1 8-ounce container whipped topping, thawed

In a 9-inch glass pie plate, mix all crust ingredients; press onto bottom and sides of plate; set aside.

In a small saucepan, sprinkle gelatin over water; let stand 1 minute. Stir over low heat until completely dissolved. Stir in lemon juice and vanilla; cool. In a bowl, mix berries and powdered sugar. Stir in gelatin mixture. Fold in whipped topping; spoon into crust. Chill well. When serving, top with blueberry sauce (see directions below). Refrigerate any leftovers immediately.

In a saucepan, mix all sauce ingredients; stir and cook 4 minutes.

Makes 8 servings.

JEAN'S PINEAPPLE-BLUEBERRY FLUFF PIE

An easy dessert to prepare...use a purchased crust if desired.

Crust
1½ cups graham cracker crumbs
¼ cup granulated sugar
⅓ cup butter, melted

Filling
1½ cups fresh blueberries, mixed with 2 tablespoons
   powdered sugar
1 20-ounce can crushed pineapple in juice (not in syrup), drained
1 3.4-ounce package pistachio flavored instant pudding mix
1 8-ounce container frozen non-dairy whipped topping, thawed

Mix all crust ingredients; press onto bottom and sides of a glass pie plate. Chill.

Sprinkle blueberries into crust. In a bowl, stir pineapple and dry pudding mix until well blended. Fold in whipped topping; spoon mixture over blueberries. Refrigerate and chill well. Store in refrigerator.

Makes 8 servings.

LEMONY FRESH BLUEBERRY CREAM PIE

Lemon filling swirled with sour cream and fresh blueberries.

1 cup granulated sugar
3 tablespoons cornstarch
1 cup whole milk
3 egg yolks, beaten
¼ cup butter
1 teaspoon finely grated fresh lemon peel
¼ cup fresh lemon juice
1 teaspoon pure vanilla extract
1 8-ounce container dairy sour cream
2 cups fresh blueberries
1 9-inch baked pastry shell, purchased or homemade
sweetened whipped cream

In a saucepan, mix sugar and cornstarch. Stir in milk, egg yolks, butter and lemon peel. Cook and stir over medium heat until mixture thickens and is bubbling; cook and stir 2 minutes. Remove from heat. Stir in lemon juice and vanilla. Pour into a glass bowl and cover with plastic food wrap. Cool in refrigerator.

Stir sour cream and blueberries into cooled mixture. Pour into baked pastry shell. Chill well. Top with sweetened whipped cream when serving. Store in refrigerator.

Makes 8 servings.

LIL' FRIED BLUEBERRY PIES

Fresh or frozen blueberries are used in these little pies.

Filling
½ cup granulated sugar
1 tablespoon cornstarch
¼ teaspoon ground cinnamon
½ cup water
2 cups blueberries

Crust
2 cups all-purpose flour
¼ teaspoon baking soda
¼ teaspoon salt
½ cup corn oil, mixed with ⅓ cup buttermilk
corn oil for frying

In a saucepan, mix sugar, cornstarch, cinnamon and water. Add blueberries. Cook and stir over medium heat until mixture comes to a boil. Cook and stir 2 minutes; set aside to cool.

Mix flour, baking soda and salt. Stir in corn oil-buttermilk mixture until dough forms a ball. Roll out dough on a floured surface to ⅛-inch thickness. Cut out ten 4½-inch circles. Place one tablespoon blueberry filling onto each. Fold dough over and seal edges with a fork.

Heat about ½ inch of corn oil in a skillet over medium heat. Fry pies, a few at a time, in hot oil until golden brown, about 1½ minutes on each side.

Makes 10 servings.

MERINGUE-CRUSTED BLUEBERRY PIE

Blueberries and cream in a meringue-soda cracker crust.

Crust
4 large egg whites
¼ teaspoon cream of tartar
1 teaspoon pure vanilla extract
1 cup granulated sugar
16 soda crackers, crushed
½ cup chopped pecans

Filling
1 cup whipping cream
⅓ cup granulated sugar
1 teaspoon pure vanilla extract
3 cups blueberries

Preheat oven to 325°.
Beat egg whites and cream of tartar until foamy. Beat in vanilla. Gradually beat in sugar until very stiff peaks form. Fold in crackers and pecans. Pour into a greased and floured 9-inch pie plate. Spread evenly over bottom and sides. Bake 35–40 minutes or until golden. Remove from oven. Cool.

In a large bowl, beat cream, sugar and vanilla until soft peaks form. Fold in blueberries. Spoon into crust. Chill. Store in refrigerator.

Makes 8 servings.

MOOSE'S BLUEBERRY-BOTTOM LEMONADE PIE

A frosty treat.

Crust
1½ cups graham cracker crumbs
3 tablespoons granulated sugar
5 tablespoons butter, melted

Filling
1½ cups frozen blueberries
1 6-ounce can frozen lemonade concentrate, partially thawed
2 cups vanilla ice cream, softened
1 8-ounce container non-dairy whipped topping, thawed

Mix all crust ingredients. Press onto bottom and sides of a glass pie plate.

Sprinkle crust evenly with blueberries.

Gradually beat ice cream into lemonade concentrate until well blended. Gently stir in whipped topping until smooth. Freeze until mixture will mound a little, then spoon mixture evenly over blueberries in prepared crust. Freeze until firm.

When serving, remove from freezer and let stand 10 minutes at room temperature for easier cutting. Store leftovers in freezer.

Makes 8 servings.

PECAN STREUSEL PEAR-BLUEBERRY PIE

The delicious streusel is the "top" crust.

1 9-inch unbaked pie crust

Filling
**5 medium-size, firm-ripe pears,
    peeled, cored and cut up**
3 tablespoons granulated sugar
2 tablespoons orange juice
⅛ teaspoon salt
1 teaspoon pure vanilla extract
2½ cups frozen blueberries
6 tablespoons all-purpose flour
6 tablespoons granulated sugar

Pecan Streusel Topping
1 cup all-purpose flour
¼ teaspoon salt
½ cup dark brown sugar, packed
½ cup lightly toasted pecan pieces
½ cup cold butter, cut up

Preheat oven to 350°.
Place crust into a 9-inch glass pie plate. Fold edges under, forming a high
rim ¾ inch above dish sides. Crimp edges decoratively. Bake until light
golden brown, about 20–25 minutes. Remove from oven.

In a large nonstick skillet, mix pears, 3 tablespoons sugar, orange juice and
salt. Stir and cook over medium heat until pears are tender; pour into a
large bowl. Add vanilla, blueberries, flour and sugar; mix well. Spoon into
crust and sprinkle with pecan streusel. Bake until bubbly, about 65 minutes. Serve lukewarm topped with whipped cream. Refrigerate.

In a food processor, blend all streusel ingredients to form coarse crumbs.

Makes 8 servings.

RHUBARB-BLUEBERRY PIE

Serve this delicious pie with vanilla ice cream.

Crust
2 cups all-purpose flour
¾ teaspoon salt
⅔ cup solid vegetable shortening
6 tablespoons ice cold water, about

Filling
1 cup granulated sugar
⅓ cup all-purpose flour
¼ teaspoon ground cinnamon
¼ teaspoon salt
2 cups fresh blueberries
2 cups rhubarb, cut into ½-inch pieces
1 teaspoon pure vanilla extract
2 tablespoons butter, cut up

Preheat oven to 425°.
Mix flour and salt; cut in shortening with a pastry blender until mixture resembles coarse meal. Stir in water a little at a time until just moistened; form two equal balls. Flatten on a floured surface and roll each into a 12-inch circle. Place one crust into a 9-inch pie pan.

Mix sugar, flour, cinnamon and salt. Add blueberries, rhubarb and vanilla; stir until well-mixed. Pour into crust. Dot with butter. Cover with remaining crust. Seal and flute edges. Cut slits in top crust. Bake 25 minutes, then reduce heat to 375° and bake about 20 minutes longer. Cool on a wire rack.

Makes 8 servings.

WALNUT-STREUSEL-APPLE-BLUEBERRY PIE

Fresh apples, dried blueberries, streusel-topped with walnuts and caramel!

1 9-inch unbaked pie crust

Filling
6 cups firm apples, peeled, cored and thinly sliced
⅓ cup dried blueberries
1 teaspoon pure vanilla extract
½ cup granulated sugar
3 tablespoons all-purpose flour
1 teaspoon ground cinnamon
¼ teaspoon salt

Streusel
1 cup brown sugar
½ cup all-purpose flour
½ cup quick-cooking oatmeal, uncooked
¼ cup chopped toasted walnuts
½ cup soft butter

Topping
½ cup coarsely chopped walnuts, toasted
⅓ cup purchased caramel topping, warmed

Preheat oven to 375°.
Line a 9-inch pie pan with unbaked pie crust; set aside. Mix apples and blueberries; drizzle with vanilla. In a separate bowl, mix remaining filling ingredients. Add to apple mixture; toss until coated. Spoon into crust. Mix all streusel ingredients until crumbly; sprinkle over filling.

Place on a baking sheet. Bake until apples are tender, about 55–60 minutes. Remove from oven. Let stand a few minutes. Top with toasted walnuts; drizzle with caramel.

Makes 8 servings.

BLUEBERRY PATCH TART

Try this winning dessert when the berries are coming in.

Crust
¾ cup butter
2 tablespoons granulated sugar
1½ cups all-purpose flour, mixed with ⅛ teaspoon salt
I egg yolk

Filling
2 cups fresh blueberries
½ cup granulated sugar
1 cup dairy sour cream
½ cup butter, melted
3 egg yolks
2 tablespoons all-purpose flour
1 tablespoon each, milk, fresh lemon juice
1 teaspoon pure vanilla extract

Preheat oven to 350°.
Beat butter and sugar until fluffy. Add flour and egg yolk; beat until combined. Form into a flattened circle; chill 2 hours. Roll out on a floured surface to an 11-inch circle. Place into a 9-inch pie pan. Bake until lightly browned, about 18 minutes. Cool completely; set aside.

Pour blueberries into baked crust. Beat all remaining filling ingredients until smooth; pour over blueberries. Bake about 1 hour or until set. Cool completely on a wire rack. Top with sweetened whipped cream when serving. Store in refrigerator.

Makes 12 servings.

BLUEBERRY-PINEAPPLE CREAM TART

A great dessert to share with friends.

Crust
1 cup all-purpose flour
½ teaspoon salt
⅓ cup plus 1 tablespoon solid shortening
3 tablespoons ice cold water, about

Topping
1½ cups whipping cream
⅓ cup powdered sugar
1 teaspoon pure vanilla extract
**1 teaspoon freshly grated
   lemon rind**

Filling
2 cups blueberries, mixed with ½ cup warm blueberry preserves
1 3-ounce package cook & serve lemon pudding and pie filling mix
½ cup granulated sugar
2 egg yolks, beaten
⅔ cup canned crushed pineapple with juice
1½ cups water
1 teaspoon freshly grated lemon rind
1 teaspoon pure vanilla extract

Preheat oven to 450°.
Mix flour and salt. Cut in shortening with a pastry blender until mixture resembles coarse meal. Stir in water until moistened; roll dough out on a floured surface to an 11-inch circle; place into a 10-inch tart pan with removable bottom (or use a pie pan). Press onto bottom and sides; trim edges. Bake 10 minutes, or until lightly browned; remove from oven; cool.

Spread bottom of baked crust evenly with blueberries-preserve mixture. In a saucepan, mix remaining filling ingredients; stir and cook, bringing to a boil over medium heat. Cool slightly, then spoon evenly over blueberries-preserve mixture. Refrigerate and chill well.

Beat cream, powdered sugar and vanilla to stiff peaks. Spread over filling; sprinkle with lemon rind. Store in refrigerator.

Makes 8 servings.

CHOCOLATE BLUEBERRY FRUITY TART

A chocolate crust holds this mixture of fruit.

Crust
1½ cups vanilla wafer crumbs
⅓ cup unsweetened cocoa powder
⅓ cup powdered sugar
½ cup butter, melted

Topping
1 8-ounce package cream cheese, softened
½ cup granulated sugar
3 tablespoons unsweetened cocoa powder
1 tablespoon whole milk
1 teaspoon pure vanilla extract

1½ cups fresh blueberries
1½ cups fresh strawberries, cut in half
3 fresh peaches, peeled and sliced
1 ripe banana, sliced
¼ cup apricot preserves

Mix crumbs, cocoa and powdered sugar. Stir in butter. Press onto bottom and side of a lightly buttered 12-inch pizza pan. Chill well.

Beat cream cheese and granulated sugar until fluffy. Add cocoa, milk and vanilla; beat until smooth. Spread mixture evenly over crust; refrigerate until chilled. Place fruit over cream cheese layer. Heat preserves until melted; cool slightly, then spoon over fruit. Chill well. Store in refrigerator.

Makes 8 servings.

FRESH BLUEBERRY-RASPBERRY TART

Fresh berries in a cookie crust.

Crust
1 cup all-purpose flour
6 tablespoons butter, softened
2 tablespoons granulated sugar
1 egg yolk

Filling
1 8-ounce package cream cheese, softened
1 teaspoon pure vanilla extract
¾ cup marshmallow creme
1½ cups fresh blueberries
1½ cups fresh raspberries

¼ cup apricot preserves
1 tablespoon water

Preheat oven to 325°.
Mix all crust ingredients with a pastry blender until a soft dough forms.
Press firmly onto a 12-inch pizza pan within ½ inch of edge. Prick all over
with a fork. Bake until golden, about 25 minutes. Cool.

Mix cream cheese, vanilla and marshmallow creme until smooth; spread
evenly over crust. Top evenly with berries.

In a small saucepan, heat preserves and water until preserves are melted.
Cool slightly. Spoon over berries. Store in refrigerator.

Makes 12 servings.

LITTLE BLUEBERRY TARTLETS

A good snack for after school.

Crust
2 cups all-purpose flour
6 tablespoons powdered sugar
¼ teaspoon salt
¼ teaspoon ground cinnamon
¾ cup butter
2 egg yolks
1 teaspoon pure vanilla extract
1 tablespoon ice cold water

Filling
½ cup granulated sugar
2 tablespoons fresh lemon juice
2 cups blueberries

Preheat oven to 350°.
Mix flour, powdered sugar, salt and cinnamon. Cut in butter with a pastry blender until crumbs form. Add egg yolks, vanilla and water; stir until blended. Gather dough into a ball, then divide into 12 equal size balls; flatten each. Refrigerate to chill. Roll each ball on a floured surface to a 5-inch round circle. Press pastry rounds into twelve 4-inch tartlet baking pans.

In a saucepan, mix sugar and lemon juice; stir over low heat until sugar is dissolved. Stir in blueberries. Remove from heat. Place equal amounts of filling in center of each tartlet pastry. Place on a large baking sheet. Bake until golden, about 20 minutes. Cool. Refrigerate leftovers.

Makes 12 servings.

RHUBARB-BLUEBERRY TART

Strawberry rhubarb and blueberries...a colorful tart.

Crust
1 cup all-purpose flour
1 tablespoon granulated sugar
¼ teaspoon salt
¼ cup butter
¼ cup solid shortening
3 tablespoons water

Filling
½ cup granulated sugar
3 tablespoons cornstarch
2 cups strawberry rhubarb, fresh or frozen, sliced into ¼-inch pieces
⅔ cup apple juice
1 cup fresh or frozen blueberries
1 teaspoon pure vanilla extract

sweetened whipped cream

Preheat oven to 375°.
Mix flour, sugar and salt. Cut in butter and shortening until crumbly. With a fork, stir in water just until moistened; gather into a ball. Roll out onto a floured surface to a 10-inch circle. Place into a 9-inch tart pan with removable bottom. Press dough onto bottom and sides. Bake 10 minutes.

In a 2-quart saucepan, mix sugar and cornstarch. Gradually stir in strawberry rhubarb and apple juice. Cook, stirring constantly, until thickened, about 7 minutes. Stir in blueberries and vanilla; pour into crust. Bake 40–50 minutes or until center is bubbly. Cool completely. Garnish top with whipped cream around edge, then criss-cross. Store in refrigerator.

Makes 8 servings.

BLUEBERRY TORTE

Lots of blueberries in this cream cheese-topped torte.

Cake
2¼ cups all-purpose flour
½ teaspoon salt
1 teaspoon baking powder
¾ teaspoon baking soda
¾ cup butter, softened
1⅔ cups granulated sugar
3 eggs
1½ teaspoons pure vanilla extract
1 cup buttermilk

Filling
2 cups granulated sugar
4 tablespoons cornstarch
1½ cups water
4 cups frozen blueberries

Topping
1 8-ounce package cream cheese
1½ cups powdered sugar
1 16-ounce non-dairy whipped topping

Preheat oven to 350°.
Mix flour, salt, baking powder and soda; set aside. Beat butter and sugar until light and fluffy. Beat in eggs, one a time. Add vanilla. Stir in flour mixture alternately with buttermilk. Pour equal amounts of batter into two greased and waxed-paper lined 9-inch cake baking pans. Bake 25 minutes or until a wooden pick inserted comes out clean. Cool completely in pans on a wire rack.

In a saucepan, stir sugar and cornstarch; stir in water. Add blueberries; stir and cook over medium heat until thickened; cool.

Beat cream cheese and sugar, then beat in whipped topping until smooth.

Cut each cake layer in half horizontally, making four layers. Place one layer cut side up on a cake plate. Spoon in ¼ filling, then ¼ topping. Repeat cake, filling and topping layers, ending with topping. Leave sides plain. Chill well. Store in refrigerator.

Makes 10 servings.

BLUEBERRY SOUR CREAM TORTE

A nice dessert for special days.

Crust
1½ cups all-purpose flour
½ cup granulated sugar
1½ teaspoons baking powder
¼ teaspoon ground cinnamon
8 tablespoons butter
1 egg
1 teaspoon pure vanilla extract

Filling
4 cups fresh blueberries
2 cups dairy sour cream
2 egg yolks, beaten
½ cup granulated sugar
1 teaspoon pure vanilla extract

Preheat oven to 350°.
Mix flour, sugar, baking powder and cinnamon. Cut in butter with a pastry blender until crumbly. Add egg and vanilla; mix well. Press onto bottom of a buttered springform pan.

Spread blueberries over crust. Mix sour cream, egg yolks, sugar and vanilla until smooth; pour over blueberries. Bake until light brown on edge, about one hour. Cool on a wire rack. Remove sides of pan. Store in refrigerator.

Makes 8 servings.

BLUEBERRY MIXED-BERRY TORTE

Blueberries, sorbet, yogurt and more fresh summer berries in this refreshing torte.

Crust
2 3-ounce packages soft ladyfingers, split
6 tablespoons raspberry juice, divided
1 pint lemon sorbet, softened
1 pint lime sorbet, softened
1 pint vanilla frozen yogurt, softened

Filling
2 cups fresh blueberries
2 cups fresh raspberries
1 cup fresh blackberries

sweetened whipped cream

Fit ladyfingers on sides and bottom of a 9-inch springform pan, trimming as necessary. Brush cut sides of ladyfingers with half the juice. Layer lemon sorbet, lime sorbet and frozen yogurt in pan. Smooth top; cover with plastic food wrap; freeze.

Place all berries in a large bowl. Stir in remaining juice until berries are coated. When serving, spoon berries on top of torte. Remove pan sides. Garnish with whipped cream as desired. Store leftovers in freezer.

Makes 8 servings.

BLUEBERRY TURNOVERS

In a cream cheese crust!

Crust
2¼ cups all-purpose flour
⅛ teaspoon salt
¾ cup butter, softened
1 8-ounce package cream cheese, softened

Filling
1 cup blueberry preserves
1 egg white, beaten

Glaze
2 tablespoons butter, melted
¾ cup powdered sugar
½ teaspoon pure vanilla extract
2 tablespoons orange juice, about

Preheat oven to 375°.
Mix flour and salt. Cut in butter and cream cheese until well mixed. Form into a ball. Roll out on a floured surface to about an ⅛-inch thickness; cut pastry into 5-inch circles.

Place 1 tablespoon blueberry preserves on half of each circle and fold over other half. Brush edges with egg white and crimp with a fork to seal. Place on a baking sheet. Brush tops with egg white. Carefully prick top two times. Bake 15–20 minutes or until light golden brown. Cool slightly, then glaze (see directions below). Serve warm or cold. Store in refrigerator.

Stir all glaze ingredients to make a smooth glaze.

Makes about 10 turnovers.

BLUEBERRY TOASTER PASTRIES

Blueberry jam is used in this recipe.

Crust
½ cup granulated sugar
½ cup vegetable shortening
2 eggs
1 teaspoon pure vanilla extract
2½ cups all-purpose flour
2 teaspoons baking powder
¼ teaspoon salt

Filling
blueberry jam or preserves

Glaze
1 egg white, beaten with
** 1 tablespoon milk**
granulated sugar

Preheat oven to 350°.
Beat sugar and shortening until light. Beat in eggs and vanilla. In another bowl, mix flour, baking powder and salt. Stir into creamy mixture to form a dough.

Divide dough equally into 16 parts; roll each into a flattened ball. Cover and chill two hours. Roll a flattened ball of dough out into a rectangle ¹⁄₁₆ inch thick. Spread one heaping teaspoon jam or preserves evenly over dough, leaving a large border uncovered on sides and ends. Roll out another ball to same shape; place on top of filling. Trim tart to a size of 3½ x 5 inches. Seal edges by crimping with a fork. Place on a greased baking sheet; prick top. Repeat with remaining flattened balls of dough.

Brush tarts with egg white mixture and sprinkle with sugar. Bake about 10 minutes; prick again with fork, keeping tarts flat. Continue baking about 15 minutes, until edges are browned. Remove from baking sheet; cool, keeping tarts flat. Wrap in plastic food wrap. Store in refrigerator.

Makes 8 toaster pastries.

LITTLE BLUEBERRY PAN PASTRIES

Especially good served with vanilla ice cream.

Pastry
2 cups all-purpose flour
2 teaspoons baking powder
½ teaspoon salt
⅔ cup solid shortening
½ cup whole milk

Syrup
½ cup granulated sugar
1 cup water
3 tablespoons butter
1 tablespoon fresh lemon juice
2 teaspoons freshly grated lemon rind

Filling
1 21-ounce can blueberry pie filling
1 teaspoon pure vanilla extract

Preheat oven to 375°.
Mix flour, baking powder and salt. Cut in shortening to form coarse crumbs; stir in milk with a fork until dough forms a ball. Divide dough in half. Roll each half into a 12-inch square. Cut into four 6-inch squares. Stir vanilla into pie filling and place about ¼ cup filling in center of each pastry square. Fold dough up around filling; pinch edges to seal well. Place onto a 13x9-inch pan. Repeat with remaining dough and filling. Bake 30–35 minutes.

In a saucepan, mix all syrup ingredients. Bring to a full boil over medium heat; pour hot syrup over pastries. Bake until pastries are golden brown and syrup is thickened, about 15–20 minutes. Serve warm with vanilla ice cream. Refrigerate leftovers.

Makes 8 pastries.

Bars
Squares
Cookies
Scones
Biscotti

APPLESAUCE-BLUEBERRY SPICE BARS

With a nutty sour cream frosting.

1 cup granulated sugar
⅓ cup butter, softened
1 egg
1 teaspoon pure vanilla extract
1½ cups all-purpose flour
1 teaspoon ground allspice
1 teaspoon ground cinnamon
¾ teaspoon baking soda
¼ teaspoon salt
1½ cups applesauce
½ cup dried blueberries
½ cup dark raisins

Frosting
2 cups powdered sugar
¼ cup dairy sour cream
2 tablespoons butter, softened
1½ teaspoons pure vanilla extract
⅓ cup chopped pecans

Preheat oven to 350°.
Beat sugar, butter, egg and vanilla until creamy. Mix flour, spices, soda and salt; add to creamed mixture. Beat in applesauce on low speed until well blended. Stir in blueberries and raisins. Spoon batter into a lightly greased 13x9-inch pan. Bake 25–35 minutes or until a wooden pick inserted in center comes out clean. Cool completely.

Beat all frosting ingredients except pecans until smooth. Frost whole pan; sprinkle with pecans. Cut into bars.

Makes 36 bars.

BANANA-BLUEBERRY
CREAM CHEESE NUT BARS

A nice bar to offer for an afternoon snack.

1 8-ounce package cream cheese, softened
1½ cups brown sugar, packed
½ cup solid margarine
1 cup ripe mashed bananas
¼ cup milk
1 egg, beaten
1 teaspoon pure vanilla extract
2¼ cups all-purpose flour
1½ teaspoons baking powder
1 teaspoon salt
1 teaspoon ground cinnamon
¾ cup chopped walnuts
½ cup dried blueberries
⅓ cup dark raisins
powdered sugar

Preheat oven to 350°.
Beat cream cheese, sugar and margarine. Stir in bananas, milk, egg and vanilla. Mix flour, baking powder, salt and cinnamon; stir into creamed mixture. Stir in walnuts, blueberries and raisins.

Pour into a greased 15x10-inch jelly roll pan. Bake 30–35 minutes or until a wooden pick inserted in center comes out clean. Cool. Sprinkle with powdered sugar. Cut into bars. Store in refrigerator.

Makes 36 bars.

BLUEBERRY BARS

A simple and tasty blueberry bar.

Crust
1 cup all-purpose flour
¾ cup brown sugar, packed
¼ cup butter or margarine

Filling
1 teaspoon ground cinnamon
¾ teaspoon baking soda
¼ teaspoon salt
½ cup sour cream
1 egg, beaten
1 teaspoon pure vanilla extract
1 cup fresh blueberries
powdered sugar

Preheat oven to 350°.
Mix flour and brown sugar; cut in butter with a pastry blender until mixture resembles coarse meal. Press 1⅓ cups onto bottom of an ungreased 8-inch square baking pan.

Mix cinnamon, baking soda and salt. Add remaining crumb mixture, sour cream, egg and vanilla; stir until well blended. Stir in blueberries. Spoon over crust; spread evenly. Bake 35 minutes. Cool in pan. Sprinkle with powdered sugar. Cut into bars.

Makes 12 bars.

BLUEBERRY FRUITCAKE BARS

Applesauce, nuts, dried and candied fruit...a nice holiday treat.

2 eggs
¼ cup butter or margarine, melted and cooled
1 14-ounce can sweetened condensed milk (not evaporated)
2 teaspoons pure vanilla extract
3 cups biscuit baking mix
1 15-ounce jar applesauce
1 cup chopped dates
1 6-ounce container red candied cherries, chopped
1 6-ounce container green candied cherries, chopped
½ cup each chopped pecans and walnuts
⅔ cup dark raisins
½ cup dried blueberries
powdered sugar

Preheat oven to 325°.
Beat eggs, butter, sweetened condensed milk and vanilla. Stir in remaining ingredients except powdered sugar. Spread into a greased and floured 15x10-inch jelly roll pan. Bake 35–40 minutes or until a wooden pick inserted in center comes out clean. Remove from oven. Cool completely. Sprinkle with powdered sugar. Cut into bars. Cover with plastic food wrap. Refrigerate leftovers.

Makes 48 bars.

BLUEBERRY GRANOLA BARS

Great for taking along on hiking trips.

¼ cup brown sugar, packed
1½ teaspoons ground cinnamon
⅛ teaspoon salt
½ cup honey
3 tablespoons vegetable oil
1½ cups quick-cooking oatmeal, uncooked
2 cups fresh blueberries

Preheat oven to 350°.
In a saucepan, mix sugar, cinnamon and salt. Add honey and vegetable oil.
Bring to a boil over medium heat. Do not stir. Boil 2 minutes.

Mix oatmeal and blueberries. Stir in honey mixture until well blended.
Spread into a 9-inch square baking dish; press flat. Bake until lightly
browned, about 40 minutes. Remove from oven; cool completely in pan
on a rack. Cut into bars.

Makes 12 bars.

COCONUT-BLUEBERRY BARS

A tasty snack.

Crust
1 cup all-purpose flour
½ cup butter, softened
¼ cup powdered sugar

Filling
2 eggs, slightly beaten
1 cup granulated sugar
½ cup flaked coconut
1 tablespoon fresh lemon juice
1 teaspoon pure vanilla extract
¼ cup all-purpose flour
½ teaspoon baking powder
½ teaspoon ground cinnamon
¼ teaspoon salt
1 cup blueberries

Preheat oven to 325°.
Mix flour, butter and powdered sugar until smooth. Spread mixture onto bottom of an 8-inch square baking pan. Bake until lightly browned, about 20–25 minutes. Remove from oven.

Mix eggs, granulated sugar, coconut, lemon juice and vanilla. Mix flour, baking powder, cinnamon and salt; stir into egg mixture. Stir in blueberries. Spread over baked crust. Bake 30 minutes. Remove from oven. Cool in pan on a wire rack. Cut into bars.

Makes 12 bars.

CHOCOLATE-TOPPED BLUEBERRY BARS

Make these bars for a special afternoon coffee.

Crust
1 cup all-purpose flour
1 cup quick-cooking oatmeal, uncooked
1½ cups granulated sugar
1¼ cups butter, softened

Filling
1 21-ounce can blueberry pie filling
1 teaspoon pure vanilla extract

Topping
½ cup semisweet chocolate chips
1 tablespoon solid shortening

Preheat oven to 350°.
Beat all crust ingredients until crumbly. Reserve 1½ cups mixture. Press remaining mixture onto bottom of a 13x9-inch pan. Bake until edges are lightly browned, about 15–20 minutes. Remove from oven, but do not cool.

Mix pie filling and vanilla. Spread over hot crust. Sprinkle evenly with reserved crumb mixture. Return to oven and bake about 30 minutes or until lightly browned. Remove from oven.

Melt chocolate and shortening; stir until smooth. Drizzle over top. Cool completely, then cut into bars.

Makes 36 bars.

CREAMY BLUEBERRY PRESERVES BARS

Cream cheese and preserves on a shortbread crust.

Crust
2 cups all-purpose flour
½ cup brown sugar, packed
½ teaspoon salt
¾ cup butter, cut up

Filling
¾ cup blueberry preserves
2 8-ounce packages cream cheese, softened
¾ cup granulated sugar
2 large eggs
1 teaspoon pure vanilla extract

Preheat oven to 350°.
Mix flour, brown sugar and salt. Cut in butter with a pastry blender until mixture forms small lumps; press mixture onto bottom of a 13x9-inch pan. Bake until golden, about 20 minutes. Remove from oven.

Spread blueberry preserves evenly over hot crust.

Beat cream cheese until smooth. Add granulated sugar, eggs and vanilla; beat until creamy; pour mixture over blueberry preserves. Bake until puffed, about 30–35 minutes. Cool completely in pan. Cut into bars. Store in refrigerator.

Makes 24 bars.

FRESH APPLE-BLUEBERRY BARS

With apricots, pecans, brown sugar and cinnamon.

6 tablespoons butter, room temperature
⅔ cup brown sugar, packed
1 teaspoon pure vanilla extract
2 large eggs
1 cup all-purpose flour
½ cup quick-cooking oatmeal, uncooked
1¼ teaspoons ground cinnamon
½ teaspoon baking powder
¼ teaspoon salt
1½ cups finely chopped cored apples
½ cup chopped dried apricots
⅓ cup dried blueberries
⅓ cup dark raisins
½ cup chopped pecans
powdered sugar

Preheat oven to 375°.
Beat butter, brown sugar and vanilla until light and fluffy. Beat in eggs one at a time.

Mix flour, oatmeal, cinnamon, baking powder and salt; gradually beat into creamy mixture on low speed. Stir in remaining ingredients except powdered sugar. Spread mixture into a greased 9-inch square baking pan. Bake 30–40 minutes or until center is firm and golden brown. Remove from oven; cool in pan. Cut into bars. Dust with powdered sugar as desired.

Makes 9 bars.

LEMON PECAN BLUEBERRY BARS

Use fresh or frozen blueberries for these bars.

1 cup butter
¾ cup powdered sugar
2 cups all-purpose flour
½ cup finely chopped pecans, divided
1½ cups blueberries, thaw if using frozen berries
4 eggs
1½ cups granulated sugar
½ cup fresh lemon juice
1 teaspoon pure vanilla extract
1 teaspoon baking powder, mixed with ¼ cup all-purpose flour

Preheat oven to 350°.
Beat butter until fluffy. Beat in powdered sugar. Gradually beat in 2 cups flour. Stir in ¼ cup pecans. Press mixture onto bottom of a lightly greased 13x9-inch pan. Bake until golden, about 20 minutes. Remove from oven; top evenly with blueberries.

Mix eggs, granulated sugar, lemon juice, vanilla and baking powder mixture. Beat on medium speed for 2 minutes. Pour mixture over blueberries. Sprinkle with remaining pecans. Bake until set and topping is lightly browned, about 30–35 minutes. Remove from oven; cool in pan. Cut into bars. Dust with additional powdered sugar. Store in refrigerator.

Makes 36 bars.

NO-BAKE CHOCOLATE-PEANUT BUTTER-BLUEBERRY GRANOLA BARS

Stir these tasty treats for the kids...you can indulge too!

3 1-ounce squares unsweetened chocolate, cut up
¼ cup peanut butter
1 14-ounce can sweetened condensed milk (not evaporated)
1 teaspoon pure vanilla extract
4½ cups granola cereal
1¼ cups flaked coconut
½ cup dried blueberries

In a large heavy saucepan, over low heat, stir chocolate, peanut butter and sweetened condensed milk until melted. Remove from heat; stir in vanilla. Stir in granola, coconut and blueberries. Pour mixture into a 13x9-inch glass dish or pan; press to flatten. Chill until set, about 2 hours. Cut into bars. Store in refrigerator.

Makes 30 bars.

OATS AND BLUEBERRY BARS

Use blueberry pie filling to make these delicious bars.

1½ cups quick-cooking oatmeal, uncooked
1½ cups all-purpose flour
1 cup brown sugar, packed
½ teaspoon ground cinnamon
¼ teaspoon baking powder
¼ teaspoon salt
¾ cup butter, softened
1 21-ounce can blueberry pie filling
1 teaspoon pure vanilla extract

Preheat oven to 375°.
In a food processor using steel blade, mix oatmeal, flour, sugar, cinnamon, baking powder and salt. Add butter; process until coarse crumbs form (or use a pastry blender to cut in butter to form crumbs). Reserve 1 cup mixture. Press remaining mixture onto bottom of a 9-inch square baking pan. Bake 5 minutes. Remove from oven.

Spoon pie filling over crust; drizzle with vanilla. Top evenly with remaining crumb mixture. Bake until top is crisp, about 25 minutes. Remove from oven; cool in pan on a wire rack. Cut into bars.

Makes 24 bars.

PERLEY BLUEBERRY-LEMON CHEESECAKE BARS

A good bar to serve for that garden club meeting.

Crust
1¼ cups all-purpose flour
¾ cup quick-cooking oatmeal, uncooked
¾ cup brown sugar, packed
½ cup chopped walnuts
½ cup margarine, cold

Filling
1 cup fresh blueberries, chopped
¼ cup fresh orange juice
2 tablespoons granulated sugar
2 teaspoons cornstarch
1 8-ounce package cream cheese, softened
2 eggs
½ cup granulated sugar
2 tablespoons fresh lemon juice
1 teaspoon freshly grated lemon peel
1 teaspoon pure vanilla extract

Preheat oven to 350°.
Mix all crust ingredients except margarine. Cut in margarine with a pastry blender until mixture resembles coarse crumbs. Reserve 1 cup crumb mixture; press remaining crumb mixture firmly onto bottom of a lightly greased 13x9-inch pan. Bake 10 minutes. Remove from oven.

In a saucepan, mix blueberries, orange juice, 2 tablespoons sugar and cornstarch; stir and cook until thickened, about 5 minutes; cool slightly and set aside.

Beat cream cheese, eggs, ½ cup sugar, lemon juice, peel and vanilla until smooth; pour into baked crust. Swirl blueberry mixture into cream cheese mixture. Top with reserved crumb mixture. Bake 25 minutes. Cool completely; cut into bars. Store in refrigerator.

Makes 36 bars.

RHUBARB-BLUEBERRY BARS

Fresh or frozen rhubarb may used.

Filling
1 cup sliced rhubarb
⅓ cup water
1 tablespoon granulated sugar
1 cup blueberry preserves
2 tablespoons cornstarch, mixed with 2 teaspoons granulated sugar
1 teaspoon fresh lemon juice
1 teaspoon pure vanilla extract

Crust
1½ cups quick-cooking oatmeal, uncooked
1¼ cups all-purpose flour
1 cup brown sugar, packed
½ teaspoon baking soda
¼ teaspoon salt
¾ cup butter, softened
¾ cup powdered sugar, mixed with 3 tablespoons orange juice

Preheat oven to 350°.
In a saucepan, mix rhubarb, water and sugar. Bring to a boil. Reduce heat; cover and cook on low until rhubarb is very soft. Mix preserves and cornstarch mixture; stir into rhubarb mixture. Cook and stir until mixture thickens and comes to a boil. Remove from heat; stir in lemon juice and vanilla.

Mix all dry crust ingredients. Cut in butter until crumbly. Reserve 1¼ cups crumb mixture. Press remaining crumb mixture onto bottom of an 8-inch square baking pan. Bake 20 minutes. Spread filling over crust; sprinkle with remaining crumbs. Bake 30 minutes. Cool in pan. Drizzle with powdered sugar mixture. Cut into bars.

Makes 16 bars.

ALI'S BLUEBERRY CHESS SQUARES

A cake mix makes this an easy dessert to prepare.

Crust
1 18-ounce box yellow cake mix
1 egg
½ cup butter, softened
1 teaspoon freshly grated lemon rind, divided

Filling
2 cups blueberries
1 tablespoon granulated sugar
2 tablespoons fresh lemon juice
1 8-ounce cream cheese, softened
2¾ cups powdered sugar
3 eggs
1 teaspoon pure vanilla extract

additional fresh blueberries and additional powdered sugar

Preheat oven to 325°.
Mix cake mix, 1 egg, butter and ½ teaspoon grated lemon rind. Pat mixture into a buttered and floured 13x9-inch pan.

Mix blueberries, granulated sugar, lemon juice and ½ teaspoon grated lemon rind; set aside. Beat cream cheese, powdered sugar, 3 eggs and vanilla until smooth. Stir in blueberry mixture. Pour over crust. Bake until set and browned, about 45–55 minutes. Cool in pan; chill. Cut into squares.

When serving, top with fresh blueberries and dust with powdered sugar as desired. Store in refrigerator.

Makes 16 servings.

BLUEBERRY KUCHEN

A nice treat to share with friends.

3 cups all-purpose flour
1¾ cups granulated sugar
4 teaspoons baking powder
½ teaspoon salt
½ cup solid margarine or shortening
1⅓ cups whole milk
2 large eggs
1 teaspoon freshly grated nutmeg
2 teaspoons freshly grated lemon rind
2 teaspoons pure vanilla extract
1½ cups chopped walnuts or pecans
3 cups blueberries
powdered sugar

Preheat oven to 350°.
Mix flour, granulated sugar, baking powder and salt. Cut in margarine until
blended. Stir in milk. Beat mixture for 3 minutes. Beat in eggs one at a time.
Add nutmeg, lemon rind and vanilla; beat 2 minutes. Stir in nuts by hand.
Fold in blueberries.

Pour batter into a greased and floured 13x9-inch pan. Bake until golden
brown, about 45 minutes. Remove from oven. Cool to room temperature.
Sprinkle with powdered sugar as desired. Cut into squares. Refrigerate
leftovers.

Makes 12 servings.

CITRUS BLUEBERRY SQUARES

Lemon, lime and blueberries.

Crust
1 cup all-purpose flour
1 tablespoon yellow cornmeal
¼ cup granulated sugar
¼ teaspoon salt
½ cup cold butter, cut up

Filling
3 eggs
¾ cup granulated sugar
2 tablespoons all-purpose flour
½ teaspoon each—freshly grated lemon and lime rind
2 tablespoons each—fresh lemon and lime juice
1 tablespoon whole milk
¼ teaspoon salt
1½ cups fresh blueberries
¼ cup apricot or peach jam, heated

Preheat oven to 375°.
Mix flour, cornmeal, sugar and salt. Cut in butter with a pastry blender until mixture resembles coarse meal. Press mixture onto bottom and an inch up the sides of a buttered 8-inch square glass baking dish. Bake until golden brown, about 15–20 minutes. Remove from oven, but do not cool.

Beat eggs, sugar, flour, rinds, juices, milk and salt. Pour immediately into hot crust; bake until just set, about 18 minutes. Spoon fresh blueberries over top; bake 3 more minutes. Cool on a wire rack. Spoon jam over top. Cover and chill. Cut into squares. Store in refrigerator.

Makes 9 servings.

MAINEE'S BLUEBERRY GINGERBREAD SQUARES

Just like Mainee...perfectly sweet and brown.

2 cups all-purpose flour
1 teaspoon baking soda
½ teaspoon salt
1 teaspoon ground cinnamon
½ teaspoon ground ginger
¼ teaspoon ground nutmeg
½ cup corn oil
1 cup granulated sugar
3 tablespoons molasses
1 egg
1 teaspoon pure vanilla extract
1 cup buttermilk
1 cup blueberries, dredged in 1 tablespoon all-purpose flour
1 tablespoon light brown sugar

Preheat oven to 350°.
Mix first 6 ingredients; set aside. Beat corn oil, sugar, molasses and egg; add vanilla. Add flour mixture to creamed mixture alternately with buttermilk; beat after each addition. By hand, stir in blueberries.

Pour mixture into a greased and floured 12x7x2-inch pan. Sprinkle with brown sugar. Bake about 35–40 minutes or until a wooden pick inserted in center comes out clean. Serve warm. Top with whipped cream if desired.

Makes 8 servings.

BLUEBERRY COOKIES

Freshly grated lemon rind lends a nice flavor to this cookie.

½ cup butter, softened
⅓ cup granulated sugar
2 egg yolks
1 teaspoon pure vanilla extract
1 teaspoon freshly grated lemon rind
1¼ cups all-purpose flour
¼ cup cornstarch
¼ teaspoon baking powder
¼ teaspoon salt
⅓ cup dried blueberries
additional granulated sugar

Preheat oven to 375°.
Beat butter and sugar until fluffy. Beat in egg yolks, vanilla and lemon rind.

Mix flour, cornstarch, baking powder and salt; gradually beat into butter mixture using low speed, until just crumbly. Stir in blueberries and form mixture into a dough; divide in half for easier handling.

Turn dough out onto a floured surface; knead until it holds together. Form into about 15 equal pieces. Roll each piece into a ball. Place balls on a parchment-lined cookie sheet. Flatten balls to ¼-inch thickness, using the bottom of a glass dipped in granulated sugar. Repeat with other half of dough.

Bake until lightly browned around edges, about 12–14 minutes. Cool on a wire rack.

Makes 30 cookies.

BLUEBERRY-CRANBERRY
CORNMEAL COOKIES

A little cornmeal in the dough.

1½ cups granulated sugar
1½ cups butter, softened
2 eggs
2 tablespoons light corn syrup
2 teaspoons pure vanilla extract
3 cups all-purpose flour
1 cup cornmeal
2 teaspoons baking powder
½ teaspoon salt
¼ teaspoon ground cinnamon
¾ cup dried blueberries
¾ cup dried cranberries
additional granulated sugar

Preheat oven to 350°.
Beat sugar and butter until creamy. Add eggs, corn syrup and vanilla; beat
until well mixed. Mix flour, cornmeal, baking powder, salt and ground cinnamon; add to creamy mixture. Beat, using low speed, until well mixed. Stir in
dried berries by hand.

Shape rounded teaspoonfuls of dough into balls; roll in additional sugar.
Place on ungreased baking sheets one inch apart; flatten a little. Bake
9–12 minutes or until edges are lightly browned. Remove from baking
sheets; cool on a wire rack.

Makes 7 dozen.

BLUEBERRY HERMITS

Sugar and spice and dried blueberries in this cookie.

½ cup margarine
½ cup granulated sugar
½ cup brown sugar, packed
2 eggs
1 teaspoon pure vanilla extract
2 cups all-purpose flour
2 teaspoons baking powder
1 teaspoon ground cinnamon
½ teaspoon ground nutmeg
¼ teaspoon ground cloves
¼ teaspoon salt
¾ cup chopped walnuts
½ cup dried blueberries
½ cup dark raisins

Preheat oven to 350°.
Beat margarine, sugars, eggs and vanilla until light and fluffy. Mix flour, baking powder, cinnamon, nutmeg, cloves and salt; stir into creamy mixture until blended.

Stir in walnuts, blueberries and raisins. Drop rounded teaspoonfuls of dough onto greased baking sheets. Bake 12–15 minutes or until lightly browned. Remove from baking sheets; cool on a wire rack.

Makes 3 dozen.

FRESH BLUEBERRY DROP COOKIES

A good cookie.

¾ cup solid margarine
1 cup granulated sugar
2 eggs
1½ teaspoons grated lemon rind
1 teaspoon pure vanilla extract
2 cups all-purpose flour
2 teaspoons baking powder
¼ teaspoon salt
½ cup whole milk
1 cup fresh blueberries

Preheat oven to 375°.
Beat margarine and sugar until fluffy. Beat in eggs, lemon rind and vanilla.

Mix flour, baking powder and salt; gradually beat into creamed mixture alternately with milk. Fold in blueberries. Drop by teaspoonfuls onto a greased baking sheet. Bake 10–12 minutes. Remove from baking sheet to a wire rack.

Makes 2½ dozen.

FROSTED BLUEBERRY DROP COOKIES

An orange-flavored frosting tops this drop cookie.

Cookies
2½ cups all-purpose flour
¾ cup granulated sugar
½ cup butter, softened
½ cup dairy sour cream
¼ cup honey
2 eggs
2 teaspoons freshly grated orange rind
1 teaspoon pure vanilla extract
½ teaspoon baking soda
½ teaspoon salt
¾ cup dried blueberries

Frosting
1½ cups powdered sugar
1 tablespoon butter, softened
¼ teaspoon pure vanilla extract
3 tablespoons fresh orange juice, about

Preheat oven to 350°.
Beat all cookie ingredients on medium except berries. Stir in blueberries.

Drop rounded teaspoonfuls of dough onto lightly greased baking sheets one inch apart. Bake 7–9 minutes. Cool completely on a wire rack, then frost. Beat butter and powdered sugar. Add vanilla and enough orange juice to make a spreading consistency.

Makes 4 dozen.

DRIED BLUEBERRY-ORANGE SCONES

Mandarin orange, blueberries, cranberries and sour cream...my favorite.

2¼ cups all-purpose flour
3 tablespoons granulated sugar
1 tablespoon baking powder
2½ teaspoons freshly grated orange peel
⅓ cup butter
½ cup mandarin orange segments, chopped
½ cup dried blueberries
½ cup dried cranberries
1 cup dairy sour cream
1 egg
2 tablespoons fresh orange juice
½ teaspoon pure vanilla extract
1 tablespoon granulated sugar

Preheat oven to 400°.
Mix flour, 3 tablespoons sugar and baking powder; stir in orange peel. Cut in butter until mixture forms coarse crumbs. Stir in mandarin oranges, blueberries and cranberries.

Beat sour cream, egg, orange juice and vanilla until smooth. Stir into flour mixture. Spread into a greased 9-inch round cake pan; smooth evenly. Sprinkle top with 1 tablespoon granulated sugar.

Bake 25–30 minutes or until a wooden pick inserted in center tests clean. Cool in pan 5 minutes. Remove from pan; cut into 8 wedges. Serve warm with soft butter.

Makes 8 scones.

MORNING FRESH BLUEBERRY SCONES

Cornmeal and buttermilk goodness in these blueberry scones.

1 cup all-purpose flour
½ cup yellow cornmeal
¼ cup granulated sugar
1 tablespoon baking powder
⅔ cup cold butter
⅓ cup buttermilk
¾ cup fresh blueberries
1 egg, beaten

Preheat oven to 375°.
Mix flour, cornmeal, sugar and baking powder. Cut in butter with a pastry blender until mixture resembles coarse meal. Stir in buttermilk. Stir in blueberries. Form a dough, adding more flour if necessary. Divide dough in half.

Turn dough out onto a floured surface. Shape each half into a 1-inch thick circle. Score each half into 4 equal wedges, but do not cut all the way through; place on a buttered baking sheet. Brush with beaten egg. Bake 20–30 minutes or until golden brown. Separate scones while warm. Serve warm with soft butter and blueberry jam!

Makes 8 scones.

PLUM LEMON-FLAVORED
BLUEBERRY SCONES

A combination of dried plums, lemon peel and dried blueberries!

2⅔ cups all-purpose flour
½ cup granulated sugar
2½ teaspoons baking powder
1 teaspoon baking soda
½ teaspoon salt
½ cup dried blueberries
1 8-ounce container lemon yogurt
⅓ cup plum puree (made with dried plums)
3 tablespoons butter, melted
1 tablespoon grated lemon peel
2 teaspoons pure vanilla extract
¼ teaspoon ground nutmeg, mixed with 2 tablespoons
  granulated sugar

Preheat oven to 400°.
Mix flour, sugar, baking powder, baking soda and salt. Stir in blueberries.

Mix yogurt, plum puree, butter, lemon peel and vanilla. Mix into flour mixture just until dough holds together.

Turn dough out onto a floured surface. Pat into a 10-inch round. Sprinkle nutmeg-sugar mixture over round; press lightly into dough. Cut round into 12 equal wedges; place on a lightly greased baking sheet 1 inch apart. Bake about 15 minutes, until browned and cracked on top. Remove from baking sheet to a wire rack. Serve warm.

Makes 12 scones.

SUGAR-TOPPED BLUEBERRY SCONES

Serve this treat with flavored butter for special mornings.

2½ cups all-purpose flour
2 teaspoons baking powder
½ teaspoon salt
½ cup cold butter, cut up
½ cup granulated sugar
¾ cup dried blueberries
¾ cup half-and-half (light cream)
1 egg
1 tablespoon grated orange rind

Topping
¼ cup granulated sugar
1½ teaspoons grated orange rind

Flavored Butter
½ cup butter, softened
2 tablespoons powdered sugar
½ teaspoon pure vanilla extract

Preheat oven to 375°.
Mix flour, baking powder and salt. Cut in butter with a pastry blender until mixture resembles small peas. Stir in sugar and blueberries. Mix half-and-half, egg and rind. Stir into flour mixture until moistened; form a dough.

Knead dough on a floured surface until smooth. Divide dough in half. Pat each half into a 7-inch circle. Place on a baking sheet. Sprinkle with topping. Score each half into 8 wedges. Bake 25–30 minutes. Cool on baking sheet 15 minutes. Separate scones while warm. Serve with flavored butter. Store any leftovers in refrigerator.

Blend all flavored butter ingredients.

Makes 16 scones.

ALMOND BLUEBERRY BISCOTTI

Dried blueberries are used in this crunchy cookie.

1 cup granulated sugar
½ cup butter, softened
¾ teaspoon almond extract
2 eggs
½ cup dried blueberries
¾ cup chopped toasted slivered almonds
2 cups all-purpose flour, mixed with 1 teaspoon baking powder
    and ¼ teaspoon salt
powdered sugar

Preheat oven to 350°.
Beat granulated sugar, butter and almond extract 2 minutes or until well-mixed. Add eggs; beat until mixture is creamy. Stir in blueberries and almonds. Gradually stir in flour mixture to form a dough.

Divide dough in half. On a lightly floured surface, shape each half into a 12x1-inch log, ½ inch thick. Place apart on a lightly greased baking sheet; flatten each to a 2-inch width. Bake until edges are light brown, about 25 minutes. Remove from oven; let stand on baking sheet 10 minutes.

Reduce heat to 300°. Using a serrated knife, cut logs diagonally into ½-inch slices. Place on same baking sheet, cut side down. Bake, turning once, about 25 minutes or until crisp and light brown on both sides. Cool completely on a wire rack. Sprinkle with powdered sugar. Store loosely covered in cookie jar.

Makes 3 dozen.

BLUEBERRY-CRANBERRY-ORANGE BISCOTTI

A good cookie.

⅔ cup granulated sugar
½ cup corn oil
1 tablespoon freshly grated orange rind
1½ teaspoons pure vanilla extract
2 eggs

2½ cups all-purpose flour
½ cup dried blueberries
½ cup dried cranberries, chopped
1 teaspoon baking powder
¼ teaspoon baking soda
¼ teaspoon salt

Preheat oven to 350°.

Mix sugar, corn oil, orange rind, vanilla and eggs until well blended. Mix remaining ingredients; stir into first mixture.

Knead dough on a lightly floured surface until smooth. Shape half the dough at a time into a 10x3-inch rectangle on an ungreased baking sheet. Bake 25–30 minutes or until a wooden pick inserted in center comes out clean. Cool on baking sheet 15 minutes. Cut the rectangle crosswise into ½-inch slices. Turn slices cut sides down on baking sheet. Bake about 15 minutes, turning once until crisp and light brown. Remove from baking sheet immediately. Cool on a wire rack.

Makes 3 dozen.

Trifles
Puddings
Other Desserts

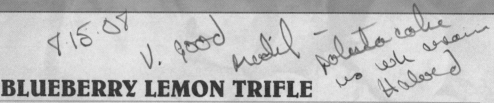

BLUEBERRY LEMON TRIFLE

Lemon custard and blueberries in this yummy trifle.

1 16-ounce pound cake, cubed

Juice
½ cup granulated sugar
⅓ cup fresh lemon juice,
   mixed with ¼ cup water

Custard
4 eggs
1 cup granulated sugar
⅓ cup fresh lemon juice
½ cup butter, cut up

Filling
4 cups fresh blueberries
¼ cup granulated sugar
1 teaspoon fresh lemon juice
1 teaspoon pure vanilla extract

Topping
2 cups whipping cream, whipped
   with 3 tablespoons granulated sugar
2 cups fresh blueberries

In a saucepan, stir and boil sugar and lemon-water mixture; reduce heat; simmer 1 minute. Cool.

In a double boiler, stir eggs and sugar. Stir in lemon juice and butter; stir and cook until thickened. Cool.

In a saucepan, stir and cook blueberries, sugar and lemon juice until thickened; stir in vanilla. Cool.

In a 3-quart glass bowl, layer in thirds, cake, juice, custard, filling and 1 cup whipped cream. Top with remaining whipped cream and fresh blueberries. Chill well before serving. Store in refrigerator.

Makes 8 servings.

SUMMER BLUEBERRY TRIFLE

A purchased angel food cake is used.

1 8-ounce package cream cheese, softened
½ cup powdered sugar
1 14-ounce can sweetened condensed milk
1 teaspoon pure vanilla extract
1 3.4-ounce package instant vanilla pudding
2 cups sweetened whipped cream, divided

1 10-inch angel food cake, cut into 1-inch pieces

4 cups fresh blueberries

Beat cream cheese and sugar. Add sweetened condensed milk, vanilla extract and dry pudding; beat well. Fold in 1½ cups sweetened whipped cream.

Arrange half of cake pieces in bottom of a large trifle bowl or any large glass bowl. Top with a layer of the creamed mixture, then with half the blueberries. Repeat layering with remaining cake pieces, cream mixture and blueberries. Spread remaining sweetened whipped cream over top; serve. Refrigerate any leftovers immediately.

Makes 6 servings.

BLUEBERRY-APPLE RICE PUDDING

Spiced with ground cinnamon.

2 eggs, beaten
½ cup granulated sugar
½ cup dairy sour cream
1 cup whole milk
1 teaspoon pure vanilla extract
½ teaspoon ground cinnamon
¼ teaspoon salt
⅓ cup dried blueberries
¼ cup dark raisins
1 apple, peeled, cored and chopped
3 cups cooked regular long grain rice (not instant)

Topping
¼ cup brown sugar, packed
1 tablespoon all-purpose flour
¼ teaspoon ground cinnamon
1 tablespoon butter, melted
sweetened whipped cream

Preheat oven to 350°.
Mix first seven ingredients until well blended. Stir in blueberries, raisins, apple and rice; mix well.

Mix all topping ingredients until well blended; sprinkle over rice mixture. Bake uncovered 45 minutes. Serve with whipped cream.

Makes 8 servings.

NELAN'S BLUEBERRY BREAD PUDDING

Blueberries and spice in a bread pudding nice.

4 cups soft white bread cubes, mixed with 1 tablespoon melted butter
2 cups fresh or frozen blueberries

Custard
3 eggs
1½ teaspoons ground cinnamon
1½ cups warm water
1 14-ounce can sweetened condensed milk (not evaporated)
¼ cup butter, melted
2 teaspoons pure vanilla extract
½ teaspoon salt

sweetened whipped cream

Preheat oven to 350°.
Place bread cubes in a buttered 9-inch square baking pan. Sprinkle with blueberries.

Beat eggs; add remaining custard ingredients; stir until well blended. Pour mixture evenly over bread and blueberries. Bake 45–50 minutes or until a knife inserted in center comes out clean. Remove from oven.

Serve warm topped with sweetened whipped cream. Refrigerate any leftovers.

Makes 8 servings.

A GOOD BLUEBERRY ICE CREAM

A dish of this ice cream is pure summertime pleasure.

4 cups fresh blueberries
1 cup granulated sugar
1 tablespoon fresh orange rind cut into strips
¼ cup water
2 tablespoons orange juice concentrate
3 tablespoons fresh lemon juice
1 teaspoon pure vanilla extract
⅛ teaspoon salt
2 cups heavy cream
1 cup half-and-half (light cream)

In a large saucepan, mix blueberries, sugar, orange strips and water. Cover and boil 5 minutes. Reduce heat and simmer uncovered 5 minutes. Discard orange strips. Puree the mixture in a blender or food processor; pour puree into a bowl. Place a fine sieve over another bowl; force mixture through.

Stir in remaining ingredients until well blended. Cover and refrigerate until chilled. Pour mixture into an ice cream maker; freeze according to the manufacturer's instructions.

Makes about 1½ quarts.

ALICE'S BLUEBERRY CLOUDS

Fresh blueberries and strawberries in a lemon-flavored cream cheese shell, garnished with fresh mint.

1 8-ounce package cream cheese, softened
½ cup granulated sugar
1 tablespoon fresh lemon juice
2 teaspoons grated lemon rind
1 teaspoon pure vanilla extract
1 cup whipping cream, whipped with 2 tablespoons
   powdered sugar
fresh blueberries
fresh strawberries, sliced
fresh mint

Beat cream cheese, sugar, lemon juice, lemon rind and vanilla. Fold in whipped cream.

Line a baking sheet with waxed paper. Shape cream cheese mixture to form ten shells with the back of a spoon; freeze.

When serving, fill frozen shells with blueberries and strawberries; garnish with fresh mint. Store leftover unfilled shells in freezer.

Makes 10 servings.

ALMOND BLUEBERRY CREPES

Dessert crepes with almond filling and orange-blueberry sauce.

Crepes
4 eggs
1 cup all-purpose flour
¼ teaspoon salt
1 cup milk
1 tablespoon light brown sugar
¼ teaspoon almond extract

Filling
1 16-ounce container cottage cheese
2 egg yolks
3 tablespoons granulated sugar
1 tablespoon freshly grated orange rind
½ cup almonds, blanched, chopped

Sauce
½ cup granulated sugar
2 tablespoons cornstarch
⅔ cup fresh orange juice
4 cups blueberries
½ teaspoon pure vanilla extract

Topping
½ cup sliced almonds,
  lightly toasted

Preheat oven to 300°.
Place all crepe ingredients into a blender; whirl until smooth. Spray a crepe pan or small nonstick skillet with vegetable cooking spray. Add 3 tablespoons batter to heated pan, tilting to make an even layer. Cook on one side until brown, about 1 minute. Place on waxed paper; repeat.

Place all filling ingredients except almonds into a blender; whirl until mixed. Add almonds; whirl until smooth.

In a saucepan, mix sugar and cornstarch. Stir in orange juice. Add blueberries; cook and stir until thickened and clear. Stir in vanilla.

To serve, place 2 rounded tablespoonfuls of filling on each crepe; roll up. Top with blueberry sauce and sprinkle with sliced almonds. Refrigerate leftovers.

Makes 18 crepes.

APPLE-BLUEBERRY DUMPLINGS

Good old-fashioned dessert.

Dumplings
2 cups all-purpose flour
1 tablespoon baking powder
½ teaspoon salt
2 tablespoons brown sugar
½ cup cold butter, cut up
¾ cup whole milk
6 apples, peeled and cored
1 cup blueberries, divided
2 tablespoons maple syrup, mixed with 1 teaspoon
  pure vanilla extract

Topping
2 cups brown sugar
1 cup water
1 teaspoon ground cinnamon
½ teaspoon ground nutmeg
¼ teaspoon dried orange peel

Preheat oven to 400°.
Mix flour, baking powder, salt and brown sugar. Cut in butter with a pastry
blender. Stir in milk to form a dough; roll out on a floured surface; cut into
six 6-inch squares; place an apple in the center of each. Place in a
greased 11x7-inch baking dish. Fill each core with blueberries. Spoon
maple syrup mixture over top. Moisten corners of dough; bring opposite
corners up over apple and pinch edges to seal well.

Heat brown sugar and water to boiling; pour around dumplings. Sprinkle
dumplings with cinnamon and nutmeg. Add dried orange peel and remaining blueberries around dumplings. Bake 45 minutes; basting often, until
crisp and browned. Serve warm with vanilla ice cream and sauce.
Refrigerate leftovers.

Makes 6 servings.

APPLE-BLUEBERRY DESSERT WRAPS

A dessert all wrapped up in a flour tortilla.

1 21-ounce apple pie filling and topping
1 cup blueberries
1 teaspoon pure vanilla extract
6 7-inch flour tortillas, warmed
3 tablespoons butter, melted
2 tablespoons granulated sugar, mixed with
   ½ teaspoon ground cinnamon
powdered sugar

In a saucepan, over medium-low heat, heat apple pie filling until warm. Stir in blueberries and vanilla; cover to keep warm.

Brush each tortilla with melted butter; sprinkle with sugar-cinnamon mixture. Spoon equal amounts of apple-berry filling down center of each tortilla. Fold bottom of tortilla to partially cover filling; fold in side to cover the filling completely. Sprinkle with powdered sugar when serving. Refrigerate leftovers.

Makes 6 wraps.

AUDREY'S BLUEBERRY DESSERT WRAPS

Fresh or frozen blueberries are wrapped in these tortillas.

Sauce
3 tablespoons granulated sugar
1½ teaspoons cornstarch
½ cup fresh orange juice
1 cup blueberries

Filling
1 8-ounce package cream cheese, softened
¼ cup powdered sugar
1 teaspoon pure vanilla extract
½ cup blueberries

8 7-inch flour tortillas
2 tablespoons butter, divided

In a saucepan, mix granulated sugar and cornstarch. Stir in orange juice; cook and stir until thickened and clear, about 5 minutes. Stir in blueberries; bring to a boil. Boil and stir 1 minute; set aside; keep warm.

Beat cream cheese until light. Add powdered sugar and vanilla; beat until smooth. Spread each tortilla with about 2 tablespoons of cheese mixture. Top with blueberries in a single row down center. Roll up like a jelly roll.

Melt 1 tablespoon butter in a skillet over medium heat. Place half of the filled tortillas seam-side down in skillet. Cook, turning, until evenly browned, about 3 minutes. Repeat with remaining butter and filled tortillas. Serve topped with warm blueberry sauce. Store any leftovers in refrigerator.

Makes 8 servings.

BLUEBERRY PARFAIT

Gingersnap cookies, lemon pudding and blueberries...a special dessert.

1 3.4-ounce package instant lemon pudding
1½ cups whole milk
1 cup heavy whipping cream, whipped to soft peaks
1 cup coarsely crushed gingersnap cookies
2 cups fresh blueberries

Prepare the pudding according to package directions using 1½ cups whole milk. Fold in whipped cream.

Spoon about a third of the pudding mixture equally into 6 serving glasses. Sprinkle lightly with half the cookie crumbs, then half the blueberries. Repeat layers, ending with pudding on top. Store in refrigerator.

Makes 6 servings.

BLUEBERRY-PEACH SLUSH

Garnish this delightful dessert with fresh mint.

1 pound ripe fresh peaches, peeled, pitted and sliced, or
**   unsweetened frozen peaches**
½ cup granulated sugar
⅓ cup water
2 teaspoons fresh lemon juice
1½ teaspoons pure vanilla extract
⅛ teaspoon ground nutmeg
½ cup dairy sour cream

2 cups fresh blueberries

Freeze sliced peaches in a single layer on a baking sheet until solid; process in a food processor with sugar, water, lemon juice, vanilla and nutmeg. Add sour cream; process until smooth.

Reserve ¼ cup of blueberries; spoon equal amounts of remaining blueberries into dessert dishes. Top with peach slush. Sprinkle with reserved blueberries. Freeze any leftovers.

Makes 4 servings.

BLUEBERRY SORBET

A light refreshing dessert.

4 cups fresh blueberries
1 6-ounce can frozen apple juice concentrate

In a food processor or blender, process blueberries and apple juice concentrate until liquefied. Pour mixture into an 11x7-inch baking dish. Cover and freeze until firm around the edges, about 2 hours.

Break frozen mixture into pieces; place into food processor or blender; process until smooth but not completely melted. Spoon mixture into a 9x5-inch food container. Cover and freeze until firm. Best served in a few days.

Makes 4 cups.

CREAMY BLUEBERRY PIZZA

Mandarin oranges and pie filling in this cheesecake pizza.

1 20-ounce package refrigerated sugar cookie dough

1 8-ounce package cream cheese, softened
⅓ cup powdered sugar
1 teaspoon pure vanilla extract
1 21-ounce can blueberry pie filling
1 11-ounce can mandarin oranges, well-drained

Preheat oven to 350°.
Cut dough into ½-inch slices; press onto a lightly greased 12-inch pizza pan, forming one large cookie. Bake until lightly browned, about 11 minutes. Remove from oven; cool.

In a bowl, beat cream cheese, powdered sugar and vanilla until smooth and fluffy; spread over crust. Top with pie filling. Garnish with oranges. Chill. Store in refrigerator.

Makes 12 servings.

EFFIE'S BLUEBERRY DESSERT

How sweet it is.

¼ cup granulated sugar
2 tablespoons cornstarch
¼ teaspoon ground cinnamon
⅛ teaspoon salt
¼ cup cold water
2 cups blueberries, thaw if frozen, reserving juice
2 teaspoons fresh lemon juice
½ teaspoon pure vanilla extract
1 frozen prepared cheesecake, thawed

In a saucepan, mix sugar, cornstarch, cinnamon and salt. Stir in water and any reserved blueberry juice; mix well. Cook and stir over medium heat until slightly thickened.

Add blueberries and lemon juice; stir and cook 4 minutes. Remove from heat. Stir in vanilla. Cool to room temperature. Spread over cheesecake; chill well. Store in refrigerator.

Makes 12 servings.

FRESH BLUEBERRY AMBROSIA

A mixture of fruit laced with lime, yogurt, coconut and pecans!

1 14-ounce can sweetened condensed milk (not evaporated)
1 8-ounce container orange yogurt
⅓ cup lime juice, fresh or from concentrate
1 cup fresh blueberries
3 oranges, peeled, sectioned, membrane removed
2 cups fresh pineapple chunks
1 cup grape halves
1 3½-ounce can flaked coconut (1⅓ cups)
1 cup miniature marshmallows
1 cup chopped pecans

In a large glass bowl, mix sweetened condensed milk, yogurt and lime juice. Gently stir in remaining ingredients. Refrigerate and chill well before serving. Spoon into dessert glasses to serve. Store in refrigerator.

Makes 10 servings.

HELEN'S BLUEBERRY DESSERT

Pineapple and blueberry pie filling in this frosty dessert.

2 8-ounce cans crushed pineapple, undrained
1 21-ounce can blueberry pie filling
1 14-ounce can sweetened condensed milk (not evaporated)
1 8-ounce container frozen non-dairy whipped topping, thawed

Topping
additional frozen non-dairy whipped topping, thawed
½ cup finely chopped pecans

Mix pineapple, blueberry pie filling and sweetened condensed milk. Fold in whipped topping. Spread evenly into a lightly buttered 13x9-inch glass baking dish. Cover and freeze until firm.

When serving, cut into squares. Garnish with whipped topping as desired. Sprinkle with pecans. Freeze leftovers.

Makes 12 servings.

LEMONY BLUEBERRY SORBET

A frozen lemonade concentrate is used in this recipe.

1 envelope unflavored gelatin
1 6-ounce can frozen lemonade concentrate, thawed
2 cups frozen blueberries
¼ cup granulated sugar
2 cups ice cubes

In a microwave-safe bowl, sprinkle gelatin over lemonade concentrate; stir. Microwave on high for 45 seconds. Stir until completely dissolved.

In a blender container, whirl blueberries, sugar and gelatin mixture until smooth. Add ice cubes; whirl until smooth.

Serve immediately as a softie, or freeze until firm for sorbet.

Makes 6 servings.

ORANGE SHERBET AND BLUEBERRIES

Simple and refreshing.

⅓ cup orange marmalade
1 pint orange sherbet
2 cups fresh blueberries

In a saucepan, heat marmalade over low heat until melted.

Scoop sherbet into four dessert dishes. Top equally with blueberries; spoon warm marmalade over top.

Makes 4 servings.

PRETZEL-CRUSTED BLUEBERRY DESSERT

Make this easy dessert for special company.

Crust
1½ cups finely crushed pretzels
¼ cup granulated sugar
½ cup butter, melted

Filling
1 14-ounce can sweetened condensed milk (not evaporated)
½ cup water
1 3.4-ounce package instant vanilla flavored pudding mix
1 4-ounce container frozen non-dairy whipped topping, thawed
1 21-ounce can blueberry pie filling

Preheat oven to 350°.
Mix all crust ingredients; press onto bottom of a 13x9-inch baking pan.
Bake 8 minutes. Cool completely.

Beat sweetened condensed milk, water and pudding mix. Fold in whipped topping. Pour mixture over cooled crust. Top with blueberry pie filling; chill. Cut into squares. Store in refrigerator.

Makes 16 servings.

PRETTY BLUEBERRY FRUIT LEATHER

A fruit roll-up "dessert" to take along—kids love it!

4 cups fresh blueberries
1 cup fresh strawberries
¼ cup honey
1 tablespoon almond extract

Process berries in a blender or food processor until smooth. Strain mixture to remove skin and seeds. Stir in honey and almond extract. Cook in a large non-stick skillet, over very low heat, stirring often, for about an hour, until thickened.

Preheat oven to 150°.
Line a large baking sheet with parchment paper; spread mixture to form a rectangle 12x8 inches. Bake with oven door slightly opened about 5 to 6 hours, or until sheet of fruit does not stick to fingers, but is moist enough to roll. Remove from oven; cool. Cut into squares. Wrap each piece in plastic food wrap; place in an air-tight container and refrigerate.

Makes about 8 pieces.

RUTH'S BLUEBERRY DESSERT

An easy dessert to prepare ahead of time for the gang.

1 8-ounce package cream cheese, softened
1 cup powdered sugar
1 teaspoon pure vanilla extract
1 8-ounce container frozen non-dairy whipped topping, thawed
1 14-ounce prepared angel food cake, cut into 1-inch cubes
2 21-ounce cans blueberry pie filling

Beat cream cheese, sugar and vanilla until smooth. Fold in whipped topping and cake cubes.

Spread mixture evenly into a 13x9-inch glass baking dish. Top evenly with blueberry pie filling. Cover; refrigerate and chill well. Cut into squares. Refrigerate any leftovers.

Makes 12 servings.

YOGURT BLUEBERRY ICE

A delicious dessert low in calories.

1 16-ounce can blueberries, undrained (not pie filling)
2 8-ounce containers low-fat vanilla yogurt
1 tablespoon honey

Process undrained blueberries in a blender or food processor until smooth; pour into a bowl. Add yogurt and honey; stir until blended. Pour mixture into an 8-inch square baking pan. Cover; freeze until firm, about 4 hours.

Break frozen mixture into pieces; place into a large bowl.

Beat with an electric mixer on medium speed until fluffy. Return mixture to same pan. Cover and freeze until firm. Scoop into ice cream dishes when serving. Store in freezer.

Makes 8 servings.

WATERMELON-BLUEBERRY COMPOTE

Strawberries and raspberries are also found in this fruity compote.

3 cups watermelon, cut into ½-inch cubes
1 cup blueberries
1 cup raspberries
1 cup strawberries, diced
3 tablespoons granulated sugar
1 tablespoon chopped fresh mint

Mix all ingredients. Let marinate 1 hour. Serve at room temperature or chilled.

Makes 8 servings.

Muffins
Pancakes
Waffles
Breads

APPLESAUCE-BLUEBERRY MUFFINS

With raisins and graham cracker crumbs in the batter.

Batter
1 cup all-purpose flour
⅔ cup graham cracker crumbs
2 teaspoons baking powder
1 teaspoon baking soda
1 teaspoon ground cinnamon
½ cup dried blueberries
½ cup dark raisins
¾ cup chunky applesauce
⅓ cup brown sugar, packed
⅓ cup margarine, melted
1 egg, beaten
1 teaspoon pure vanilla extract

Streusel Topping
¼ cup all-purpose flour
2 tablespoons brown sugar, mixed
  with ½ teaspoon ground cinnamon
2 tablespoons cold butter
⅓ cup chopped walnuts

Preheat oven to 400°.
Mix first seven batter ingredients. Mix remaining batter ingredients and stir into first mixture until just moistened. Spoon batter equally into paper-lined muffin cups. Sprinkle with streusel (see directions below). Bake about 18–20 minutes. Cool on a wire rack.

In a bowl, combine flour and sugar-cinnamon; cut in butter with pastry blender until crumbly; stir in walnuts.

Makes 12 muffins.

BANANA-BLUEBERRY MUFFINS

Ripe bananas and fresh blueberries with a lemon-flavored topping.

Dry Ingredients
2¼ cups all-purpose flour
2 teaspoons baking powder
½ teaspoon salt
½ teaspoon ground cinnamon

Wet Ingredients
2 ripe bananas, mashed
2 eggs, beaten
1 cup brown sugar, packed
½ cup margarine, melted
1 teaspoon pure vanilla extract
1 cup fresh or frozen blueberries

Topping
¼ cup granulated sugar, mixed with 1 teaspoon
freshly grated lemon rind

Preheat oven to 400°.
Mix all dry ingredients. Beat all wet ingredients, except blueberries, until blended; stir mixture into dry ingredients until just moistened, but batter is lumpy. Fold in blueberries.

Spoon batter equally into greased or paper-lined muffin cups. Sprinkle with topping mixture. Bake 20–25 minutes. Remove from pan; cool on a wire rack.

Makes 12 muffins.

BLUEBATTER BLUEBERRY MUFFINS

Crushed and whole berries in a tasty butter batter.

2 cups all-purpose flour
2½ teaspoons baking powder
½ teaspoon salt
½ cup butter, softened
1 cup granulated sugar
¼ teaspoon ground cinnamon
2 large eggs
½ cup whole milk, mixed with 1 teaspoon pure vanilla extract
½ cup crushed fresh blueberries
2 cups fresh blueberries

1 tablespoon granulated sugar

Preheat oven to 400°.
Mix flour, baking powder and salt. Beat butter, sugar and cinnamon until light and fluffy. Beat in eggs, one at a time; stir in milk. Stir mixture into dry ingredients until just moistened. Fold in crushed and whole blueberries.

Spoon batter evenly into paper-lined muffin cups. Sprinkle tops equally with 1 tablespoon granulated sugar. Bake 25–30 minutes. Cool on a wire rack.

Makes 12 to14 muffins.

BLUEBERRY CORN MUFFINS

A little honey in the batter.

Dry Ingredients
1⅓ cups all-purpose flour
1 cup yellow cornmeal
2 tablespoons granulated sugar
1 tablespoon baking powder
¾ teaspoon salt

Wet Ingredients
¾ cup whole milk
3 tablespoons honey
¼ cup margarine, melted and cooled
1 large egg, beaten
¾ cup fresh blueberries

Preheat oven to 400°.
Mix all dry ingredients. Mix all wet ingredients except blueberries until well blended; stir into dry mixture until just moistened. Stir in blueberries.

Spoon batter equally into well greased or paper-lined muffin cups. Bake 20–25 minutes. Cool in cups 5 minutes; remove from cups to a wire rack. Best served warm.

Makes 12 muffins.

BLUEBERRY CREAM CHEESE MUFFINS

Almost dessert.

Dry Ingredients
2 cups cake flour
¾ cup granulated sugar
1½ teaspoons baking powder
½ teaspoon baking soda
¼ teaspoon salt

Wet Ingredients
1 3-ounce package cream cheese, softened
2 eggs
2 teaspoons fresh lemon juice
2 teaspoons pure vanilla extract
¼ cup butter, melted
½ cup whole milk
1 cup blueberries

Preheat oven to 350°.
Mix dry ingredients. Beat cream cheese until fluffy. Beat in eggs. Stir in lemon juice, vanilla, butter and milk until well blended. Stir into dry mixture. Fold in blueberries.

Spoon batter into greased or paper-lined muffin cups. Bake 30 minutes. Remove from cups to a rack. Store in refrigerator.

Makes 12 to 14 muffins.

BLUEBERRY-ORANGE MUFFINS

Serve these muffins warm with orange marmalade.

Dry Ingredients
1⅓ cups all-purpose flour
1 cup quick-cooking oatmeal, uncooked
1 teaspoon baking powder
½ teaspoon baking soda
½ teaspoon ground cinnamon
½ teaspoon salt

Wet Ingredients
¼ cup margarine, melted and cooled
⅓ cup brown sugar, packed
1 large egg, beaten
⅔ cup milk
⅓ cup fresh orange juice
2 teaspoons freshly grated orange rind
1 teaspoon pure vanilla extract
¾ cup fresh blueberries

Preheat oven to 400°.
Mix all dry ingredients. Mix all wet ingredients, except blueberries, until well blended; stir into dry mixture until just moistened. Stir in blueberries.

Spoon batter into paper-lined muffin cups, filling ⅔ full. Bake 20–25 minutes. Remove from cups to a wire rack. Serve warm.

Makes 12 to 14 muffins.

CAKEY BLUEBERRY MUFFINS

Muffin or cake...you decide.

1 18-ounce package yellow cake mix
3 eggs
1 teaspoon ground cinnamon
½ teaspoon ground nutmeg
¼ teaspoon ground cloves
1 21-ounce can blueberry pie filling

Preheat oven to 350°.
Beat all ingredients on medium speed until blended. Spoon batter into 24 paper-lined muffin cups.

Bake 25–30 minutes or until a knife inserted in center comes out clean. Remove from pan; cool on a wire rack.

Makes 24 muffins.

CARROT-BLUEBERRY MUFFINS

Oats, raisins and walnuts mixed in with carrots and blueberries.

Dry Ingredients
1 cup all-purpose flour
1 cup quick-cooking oatmeal, uncooked
⅓ cup brown sugar, packed
2 teaspoons baking powder
1 teaspoon baking soda
1 teaspoon ground cinnamon
⅓ cup chopped walnuts

Wet Ingredients
1 cup buttermilk
⅓ cup light molasses
3 tablespoons corn oil
1 egg, beaten
1 teaspoon pure vanilla extract
1 cup fresh blueberries
1 cup freshly grated carrots
½ cup dark raisins

Preheat oven to 400°.
Mix all dry ingredients until well blended. Mix buttermilk, molasses, corn oil, egg and vanilla. Stir into flour mixture until just moistened. Stir in blueberries, carrots and raisins. Spoon batter into paper-lined muffin cups. Bake 20–25 minutes or until a wooden pick inserted in center comes out clean. Remove from pan; cool on a wire rack.

Makes 18 muffins.

DRIED BLUEBERRIES AND RAISIN MUFFINS

Yet another tasty muffin.

½ **cup brown sugar, packed**
¼ **cup solid margarine**
1 **egg**
¾ **cup pineapple juice**
½ **teaspoon pure vanilla extract**
1 **teaspoon grated orange rind**
2 **cups all-purpose flour**
1½ **teaspoons baking powder**
½ **teaspoon baking soda**
¼ **teaspoon salt**
½ **teaspoon ground cinnamon**
¼ **teaspoon ground nutmeg**
¾ **cup dried blueberries**
¼ **cup dark raisins**

Preheat oven to 375°.
Beat sugar and margarine until light and fluffy. Beat in egg. Stir in pineapple juice, vanilla and orange rind.

Mix remaining ingredients except blueberries and raisins; stir into creamy mixture until just moistened. Stir in blueberries and raisins. Spoon batter equally into greased or paper-lined muffin cups. Bake 20–25 minutes. Remove from cups; cool on a wire rack.

Makes 12 muffins.

FAVORITE OAT BRAN BLUEBERRY MUFFINS

This recipe is adapted from my book *The Muffins Are Coming*.

Dry Ingredients
⅔ cup oat bran
1¾ cups all-purpose flour
½ cup granulated sugar
1 tablespoon baking powder
¾ teaspoon salt
3 tablespoons non-fat dry milk

Wet Ingredients
¾ cup milk
1 teaspoon pure vanilla extract
1 whole egg, plus 1 white, beaten
¼ cup margarine or butter, melted and cooled slightly
1¼ cups frozen blueberries, do not thaw

Preheat oven to 400°.
Mix all dry ingredients. Mix all wet ingredients except blueberries; stir into dry ingredients until just moistened, but batter is lumpy; fold in blueberries. Spoon batter equally into paper-lined muffin cups. Bake 20–25 minutes. Remove from pan; cool on a wire rack. Serve warm.

Makes 12 muffins.

LEMON-FLAVORED BLUEBERRY MUFFINS

Sour cream adds a nice texture.

1½ cups all-purpose flour
1 teaspoon baking soda
½ teaspoon salt
½ cup granulated sugar
¼ cup butter, softened
1 cup dairy sour cream
1 egg
2 tablespoons fresh lemon juice
1 teaspoon pure vanilla extract
1 teaspoon freshly grated lemon rind
1 cup blueberries

Topping
1 tablespoon granulated sugar, mixed with ½ teaspoon freshly grated lemon rind

Preheat oven to 375°.
Mix flour, soda and salt. Beat ½ cup sugar and butter until creamy. Add next five ingredients; beat until blended; stir mixture into dry ingredients until just moistened, but batter is lumpy. Stir in blueberries.

Spoon batter equally into greased or paper-lined muffin cups. Sprinkle equally with topping. Bake 20–25 minutes. Remove from pan; cool on a wire rack.

Makes 12 muffins.

OATS AND BLUEBERRY MUFFINS

A tasty treat for afternoon tea.

1¾ cups all-purpose flour
¾ cup quick-cooking oatmeal, uncooked
1 tablespoon baking powder
½ teaspoon salt
⅔ cup granulated sugar
¼ teaspoon ground cinnamon
⅓ cup butter, melted
1 egg, beaten
1 cup whole milk
1 teaspoon pure vanilla extract
1½ cups fresh blueberries

Preheat oven to 400°.
Mix flour, oatmeal, baking powder, salt, sugar and cinnamon. Mix butter, egg, milk and vanilla; stir into dry mixture until just moistened, but batter is lumpy. Fold in blueberries.

Spoon batter equally into greased or paper-lined muffin cups. Bake 20–25 minutes. Remove from cups; cool on a wire rack.

Makes 12 to 16 muffins.

ORANGE-BLUEBERRY BRAN MUFFINS

A good choice for breakfast.

1 cup all-bran cereal (not flakes)
½ cup fresh orange juice
½ cup light brown sugar
½ teaspoon salt
½ cup sour cream
1 large egg, beaten
¼ cup corn oil
½ teaspoon pure vanilla extract
1 tablespoon freshly grated orange rind
1 cup all-purpose flour
2 teaspoons baking powder
½ teaspoon baking soda
½ cup dried blueberries

Preheat oven to 400°.
Mix bran and orange juice. Stir in sugar and salt; set aside 10 minutes.

Mix sour cream, egg, oil, vanilla and orange rind; stir into bran mixture. Mix flour, baking powder, baking soda and dried blueberries; stir into bran mixture until just moistened.

Spoon batter equally into greased or paper-lined muffin cups. Bake 20–25 minutes. Cool on a wire rack.

Makes 12 muffins.

WILD RICE BLUEBERRY MUFFINS

Minnesota produce.

Dry Ingredients
1½ cups all-purpose flour
½ cup granulated sugar
2 teaspoons baking powder
1 teaspoon ground coriander
½ teaspoon salt

Wet Ingredients
¼ cup margarine, melted and cooled
2 eggs, slightly beaten
½ cup whole milk
**1 cup frozen blueberries, coated with 1 tablespoon
  all-purpose flour**
1 cup cooked wild rice

Preheat oven to 400°.
Mix all dry ingredients. Mix margarine, eggs and milk; stir into dry mixture until just moistened. Stir in blueberries and rice.

Spoon batter into greased or paper-lined muffin cups. Bake 20–25 minutes. Remove from cups to a wire rack. Serve warm.

Makes 12 muffins.

BLUEBERRY CINNAMON PANCAKES

Serve warm with plenty of butter and maple syrup.

2 cups all-purpose flour
1 tablespoon baking powder
¼ cup granulated sugar
1 teaspoon salt
½ teaspoon ground cinnamon
1½ cups whole milk
¼ cup margarine, melted and cooled
2 eggs, lightly beaten
1¼ cups fresh blueberries

Mix flour, baking powder, sugar, salt and cinnamon. Mix milk, margarine and eggs; stir into dry mixture until blended. Stir in blueberries.

Heat a greased griddle until a drop of water sizzles. Pour ¼ cup batter onto griddle; cook until bubbles that formed on the outside edges are broken; turn pancake over; cook other side. Repeat with remaining batter.

Makes 8 to 12 pancakes.

BLUEBERRY OAT PANCAKES

Oatmeal, brown sugar and blueberries.

1 cup quick-cooking oatmeal, uncooked
2 tablespoons light brown sugar
1 cup all-purpose flour
1 tablespoon baking powder
¾ teaspoon salt
2 cups whole milk
1 large egg, beaten
3 tablespoons margarine, melted
1 cup fresh blueberries

In a blender, whirl oatmeal until fine. Add sugar; whirl. Pour mixture into a large bowl. Add flour, baking powder and salt; mix until blended.

Mix milk, egg and margarine; stir into dry mixture until moistened, but batter is lumpy. Stir in blueberries.

Heat a greased griddle until a drop of water sizzles. Pour ¼ cup batter onto griddle; cook until the bubbles that formed around the outside edge are broken. Turn pancake over; cook other side. Repeat. Add additional milk to batter if necessary for a pourable consistency.

Makes 12 pancakes.

V.V. good & V. EASY

BLUEBERRY-PEACH OVEN PANCAKES

Pancakes will go flat after baking, forming a bowl to fill with fruit.

Pancakes
¼ cup all-purpose flour
¼ teaspoon salt
1 whole egg plus 1 egg white
¼ cup milk
1 tablespoon corn oil
1 cup fresh blueberries
1 cup fresh sliced peaches, mixed with 2 tablespoons
   warm marmalade

Syrup
1 cup blueberries
½ cup maple syrup

Preheat oven to 400°.
Beat flour, salt, egg and egg white, milk and corn oil until smooth.

Spoon equal amounts of batter into four 4½-inch foil tart pans coated with vegetable cooking spray. Bake until brown and puffy, about 25 minutes. Remove from oven; place on a plate.

Mix blueberries and peach mixture; spoon into center of each pancake. Serve immediately with warm blueberry syrup below.

In a saucepan, heat blueberries and maple syrup 3 minutes; strain and pour syrup into a small pitcher.

Makes 4 pancakes.

BLUEBERRY SOUR CREAM PANCAKES

Serve these pancakes topped with butter and warm syrup.

Pancakes
1 cup all-purpose flour
2 teaspoons baking powder
1 teaspoon baking soda
¼ teaspoon salt
2 tablespoons granulated sugar
1 cup whole milk
½ cup dairy sour cream
1 egg
2 tablespoons butter, melted
1 cup fresh blueberries

Syrup
1 cup blueberries
½ cup maple syrup

Mix flour, baking powder, baking soda, salt and sugar until blended. Add all remaining pancake ingredients except blueberries. Beat until well blended. Stir in blueberries.

Heat a greased griddle until a drop of water sizzles. Pour ¼ cup batter onto griddle; cook until bubbles form, about 2–3 minutes. Turn pancake over and cook until light brown, about 1–2 minutes. Serve warm with syrup below.

In a saucepan, heat blueberries and syrup for 3 minutes; strain through a sieve; discard pulp; pour into a pitcher. Serve warm.

Makes 15 pancakes.

BLUEBERRY WAFFLES

Serve with warm blueberry sauce.

1¾ cups all-purpose flour
½ cup granulated sugar
1½ teaspoons baking powder
½ teaspoon baking soda; ½ teaspoon salt
½ teaspoon ground cinnamon
3 large eggs, separated
1 cup whole milk
¼ cup butter, melted; 2 tablespoon corn oil
1 teaspoon pure vanilla extract
1 cup plain unflavored yogurt
1 cup fresh blueberries

Mix first six ingredients. Beat egg yolks, milk, butter, corn oil and vanilla; stir in yogurt. Stir into dry mixture. Whip egg whites to soft peaks; fold into batter.

Heat waffle iron; spray with vegetable cooking spray. Pour batter in center of hot iron and spread a little; scatter ¼ cup blueberries over batter. Close iron; cook about 3–4 minutes. Remove waffle; repeat.

Blueberry sauce: In a saucepan bring 1 pound frozen blueberries, ½ cup apple juice and ½ cup granulated sugar to a boil. Reduce heat; simmer until mixture is reduced to 2 cups, about 15 minutes. Dissolve 1 tablespoon cornstarch into 2 tablespoons apple juice; stir into mixture. Bring to a boil; simmer until thickened. Stir in 1 tablespoon fresh lemon juice and ¼ teaspoon pure vanilla extract. Store in refrigerator.

Makes 4 waffles.

JOHN'S BLUEBERRY WAFFLES

Adapted from a Perley, Minnesota, recipe.

1¾ cups all-purpose flour
2 teaspoons baking powder
1 tablespoon granulated sugar
½ teaspoon salt
3 eggs
7 tablespoons melted butter
1½ cups whole milk
blueberries (about 1 cup)

Mix flour, baking powder, sugar and salt. Add remaining ingredients except blueberries. Beat well.

Heat waffle iron; spray with vegetable cooking spray. Pour about ⅓ cup batter in center; sprinkle with 2 tablespoons blueberries. Close iron; cook until crisp, about 2–3 minutes. Remove waffle; repeat. Add more milk to batter, a little at a time, if batter seems too stiff.

Serve with soft butter and warm maple syrup.

Makes about 8 waffles.

BLUEBERRY CORN BREAD

Serve warm with soft butter and honey.

1 cup all-purpose flour
¾ cup cornmeal
3 tablespoons granulated sugar
2 teaspoons baking powder
¾ teaspoon salt
1 large egg
⅔ cup milk
⅓ cup corn oil
1 cup blueberries, fresh or frozen

Preheat oven to 425°.
Mix flour, cornmeal, sugar, baking powder and salt. Beat egg; add milk and corn oil. Pour into flour mixture; stir until moistened. Fold in blueberries.

Pour batter into a greased 8-inch square baking pan. Bake about 25 minutes or until golden. Remove from oven; cut into squares.

Makes 9 servings.

BLUEBERRY DROP BISCUITS

No need to roll these out.

2 cups all-purpose flour
2 tablespoons granulated sugar
1 tablespoon baking powder
¾ teaspoon salt
¼ teaspoon ground nutmeg
1 cup whole milk
¼ cup margarine, melted and cooled
1 cup fresh blueberries

Preheat oven to 400°.
Mix flour, sugar, baking powder, salt and nutmeg. Mix milk and margarine.
Add blueberries; stir into dry mixture with a fork until dough holds together.

Drop by large tablespoonfuls onto a lightly greased baking sheet. Bake
until browned, about 15–18 minutes. Remove from pan. Serve warm.

Makes 16 biscuits.

BLUEBERRY-BANANA QUICK BREAD

An all-time favorite.

⅔ **cup granulated sugar**
½ **cup margarine**
2 eggs
¼ **cup dairy sour cream**
2 large ripe bananas, well-mashed
1 teaspoon pure vanilla extract
1 cup all-purpose flour
⅓ **cup whole wheat flour**
2 teaspoons baking powder
1 teaspoon baking soda
¼ **teaspoon salt**
1½ **cups blueberries**

Preheat oven to 350°.
Beat sugar and margarine until light and fluffy. Beat in eggs. Stir in sour cream, bananas and vanilla until well blended.

Mix flours, baking powder, soda and salt. Stir into creamy mixture; mix well. Fold in blueberries. Pour mixture into a greased 9x5-inch loaf pan.

Bake about an hour or until a wooden pick inserted in center comes out clean. Cool 5 minutes. Loosen sides of loaf from pan; remove from pan. Cool completely on a rack. Wrap in plastic food wrap; store in refrigerator.

Makes 1 loaf.

BLUEBERRY BREAKFAST ROLLS

Purchased dough will make these orange-glazed rolls an easy treat.

Filling
2 tablespoons granulated sugar
2 teaspoons cornstarch
2 tablespoons orange juice
¾ cup blueberries, finely chopped
1 teaspoon freshly grated orange rind
½ teaspoon pure vanilla extract

Glaze
1 cup powdered sugar
2 tablespoons orange juice, about
½ teaspoon pure vanilla extract

1 10-ounce can refrigerated pizza crust dough

Preheat oven to 375°.
In a saucepan, mix sugar and cornstarch. Stir in orange juice. Add blueberries and orange rind; cook over medium heat, stirring constantly, until thickened and bubbly, about 3 minutes. Stir in vanilla. Remove from heat; cool 10 minutes.

Pat out pizza dough on a floured surface into a 12x9-inch rectangle. Spread filling to within a ½ inch of border along sides. Start with long end and roll up like a jelly roll. Pinch side seam to seal, but do not seal ends. Cut into twelve 1-inch slices. Place cut-side up in greased muffin cups. Bake about 15 minutes or until lightly browned. Remove from pan; cool on a wire rack 10 minutes before glazing.

In a bowl, mix glaze ingredients to a desired consistency; drizzle over rolls.

Makes 12 rolls.

BLUEBERRY-STUFFED FRENCH TOAST

French toast from the oven, served with blueberry-orange sauce.

6 large eggs
1 teaspoon finely grated orange rind
⅔ cup fresh orange juice
½ teaspoon pure vanilla extract
2 tablespoons granulated sugar
¼ teaspoon salt
¼ teaspoon ground cinnamon
8 slices Italian bread cut 1¼ inch thick
1 cup blueberries, mixed with
   1 tablespoon granulated sugar

⅓ cup sliced almonds, toasted

Sauce
¼ cup water
¼ cup orange juice
1 cup blueberries
1 cup orange sections,
   membranes removed
3 tablespoons granulated sugar
1 tablespoon cornstarch

Preheat oven to 400°.
Beat eggs, orange rind, orange juice, vanilla, sugar, salt and cinnamon until well blended; pour into a 13x9-inch glass baking dish; set aside.

Using tip of sharp knife, cut a 1½-inch pocket in side of each bread slice. Fill pockets equally with blueberry mixture; place filled bread into egg mixture. Let stand, turning once to absorb mixture, about 5 minutes on each side. Place egg-bread onto a large baking sheet sprayed with vegetable cooking spray. Bake about 15 minutes, turning once after 10 minutes. Serve warm with sauce; top with toasted almonds.

In a saucepan, bring water and orange juice to a boil. Add blueberries and orange sections. Cook and stir 3 minutes. mix sugar and cornstarch; add to mixture, stirring constantly until sauce is thickened, about 1 minute.

Makes 8 servings.

BLUEBERRY LEMON QUICK BREAD

Slice thin and serve with a special cup of tea.

2 cups all-purpose flour
2 teaspoons baking powder
½ teaspoon salt
½ cup butter, softened
1 cup granulated sugar
1 teaspoon pure vanilla extract
2 large eggs
½ cup whole milk
1½ cups blueberries
¼ cup fresh lemon juice, mixed with 5 tablespoons
    granulated sugar

Preheat oven to 350°.
Mix flour, baking powder and salt; set aside. Beat butter and sugar until light and fluffy. Add vanilla. Beat in eggs, one at a time, on low speed, until well blended. Stir in flour mixture and milk alternately, mixing until just blended. Fold in blueberries. Spoon batter into a greased and floured 9x5-inch loaf pan.

Bake about an hour or until a wooden pick inserted in center comes out clean. Remove from oven; cool in pan 10 minutes. Remove from pan.

With a wooden pick, prick sides and top of warm loaf. Brush with lemon juice-sugar mixture. Cool on a wire rack.

Makes 1 loaf.

BLUEBERRY MACHINE BREAD

Dried blueberries are used.

¾ **cup whole milk**
1 **egg**
3 **tablespoons water**
½ **teaspoon pure vanilla extract**
2 **tablespoons margarine, cut up**
3 **cups bread flour**
3 **tablespoons granulated sugar**
¾ **teaspoon salt**
¼ **teaspoon ground nutmeg**
1 **teaspoon active dry yeast**
⅓ **cup dried blueberries**

Glaze
½ **cup powdered sugar**
2 **teaspoons orange juice, about**

Place all ingredients except powdered sugar and orange juice in pan of a
1½ or 2-pound bread machine according to manufacturer's instructions.
Select the basic white bread cycle. When bread is done, remove to a wire
rack. Cool.

Mix powdered sugar and orange juice to a desired consistency; drizzle
over bread.

Makes 1 loaf.

CINNAMON-SWIRL BLUEBERRY BREAD

Dried blueberries and ground cinnamon in this tasty bread.

4 to 5 cups all-purpose flour, divided
1 cup quick-cooking oatmeal, uncooked
¼ cup non-fat dry milk
2 packages active dry yeast
2 teaspoons salt
1½ cups water
½ cup light molasses
2 tablespoons corn oil
1 egg
2 tablespoons butter, melted
3 tablespoons granulated sugar, mixed with 1½ teaspoons
  ground cinnamon
1½ cups dried blueberries

Mix 1 cup flour, oatmeal, dry milk, yeast and salt. Heat water, molasses and corn oil until very warm, 120–130°. Stir into flour mixture. Add egg; beat on low speed 3 minutes. Stir in 3 cups flour by hand, a little at a time. Turn dough onto a floured surface; knead about 7 minutes until smooth and elastic, using more flour as necessary. Place dough into a greased bowl; cover with greased waxed paper; let rise until doubled in size, about 1 hour.

Punch down dough and divide into two equal portions. Roll each into a rectangle, 8x16 inches. Brush with melted butter and sprinkle with sugar-cinnamon mixture. Sprinkle with blueberries. Starting with the short end, roll up tightly. Place seam-side down into two greased 8½ x 4½-inch loaf pans. Cover; let rise until doubled, about 1 hour.

Preheat oven to 375°. Bake 40–45 minutes until golden brown and sounds hollow when tapped. Remove from pans. Cool on a wire rack.

Makes 2 loaves.

Salads
Soups

BLUEBERRY-APPLE SALAD

With grapes, walnuts and a sour cream dressing.

Salad
2 apples, peeled, cored and cubed ½ inch
2 teaspoons fresh lemon juice
½ cup dried blueberries
½ cup seedless green grapes, halved
½ cup coarsely chopped walnuts
½ cup chopped celery
½ cup miniature marshmallows

Good
7·31·08

Dressing
⅔ cup dairy sour cream
⅓ cup mayonnaise

CREAM CHEESE + HONEY
+ PINEAPPLE

Mix sour cream with mayonnaise; refrigerate.

In a large glass bowl, toss apples with lemon juice. Add remaining salad ingredients. Add dressing; toss until coated. Cover and chill at least 1 hour before serving. Store in refrigerator.

Makes 8 servings.

BLUEBERRY CHICKEN SALAD

Serve this salad on crisp lettuce leaves.

4 cups diced cooked chicken breast
1 cup dried blueberries
½ cup toasted slivered almonds
½ cup mayonnaise
¼ cup dairy sour cream
1 tablespoon fresh lemon juice
¼ cup chutney
½ teaspoon salt
⅛ teaspoon ground black pepper

In a serving bowl, mix chicken, blueberries and almonds.

Mix remaining ingredients; stir into chicken mixture. Chill well. Serve on lettuce leaves. Refrigerate leftovers.

Makes 6 servings.

BLUEBERRY CREAM CHEESE SALAD

A delicious gelatin salad.

1 6-ounce package raspberry-flavored gelatin
2 cups boiling water
1½ cups cold water
2 cups blueberries, or 2 cups canned blueberry pie filling
1 8-ounce can crushed pineapple, undrained
2 ripe bananas, sliced
1 8-ounce package cream cheese, softened
1 8-ounce container dairy sour cream
½ cup granulated sugar
1 teaspoon pure vanilla extract
½ cup coarsely chopped pecans

Stir gelatin into boiling water until dissolved; stir in cold water. Stir in blueberries and pineapple. Pour into a 13x9x2-inch glass baking dish. Chill until almost set, then stir in bananas. Chill until firmly set.

Mix cream cheese, sour cream, sugar and vanilla until smooth; spread evenly over set gelatin. Sprinkle with pecans. Store in refrigerator.

Makes 10 servings.

BLUEBERRY-LEMON GELATIN SALAD

Blueberry pie filling in this salad.

1 3.5-ounce package lemon-flavor gelatin
1 cup boiling water
1 21-ounce can blueberry pie filling
2 tablespoons fresh lemon juice
½ cup dairy sour cream
1 tablespoon granulated sugar

Mix gelatin into boiling water until dissolved; cool. Stir in pie filling and lemon juice. Chill until partially set. Spoon half the mixture into an 8½x4½ glass loaf dish. Chill until set. Keep remaining gelatin mixture at room temperature.

Mix sour cream and sugar. Spread evenly over chilled set gelatin. Top with remaining gelatin mixture. Refrigerate until firm. Cut into squares; serve on crisp salad greens.

Makes 6 servings.

BLUEBERRY LETTUCE SALAD

No tomatoes needed.

1 small head lettuce, shredded
1¼ cups blueberries, divided

Dressing
2 tablespoons white vinegar
2 tablespoons red wine vinegar
2 tablespoons fresh lemon juice
2 tablespoons olive oil
1½ teaspoons granulated sugar
1 teaspoon crushed dried basil
1 teaspoon freshly grated lemon rind
¼ teaspoon salt
⅛ teaspoon ground black pepper

2 ounces crumbled blue cheese

In a large salad bowl, mix lettuce and 1 cup blueberries.

Mix all dressing ingredients until well blended; add to salad bowl and toss
to mix. Top with blue cheese and ¼ cup blueberries. Serve immediately
or refrigerate.

Makes 4 servings.

BLUEBERRY MUSHROOM SALAD

A nice tossed salad.

4 cups mixed salad greens, torn
1 cup fresh blueberries
1 cup fresh mushrooms, sliced
4 cherry tomatoes, whole

Dressing
⅓ cup fresh orange juice
1 tablespoon olive oil
1 tablespoon brown mustard
1 teaspoon granulated sugar
1 teaspoon chopped fresh mint
¼ teaspoon salt
⅛ teaspoon ground black pepper

1 tablespoon sliced toasted almonds

V. good
8-15-08

In a large glass serving bowl, mix salad greens, blueberries, mushrooms and cherry tomatoes.

Mix all dressing ingredients until well blended. Spoon over salad. Toss with toasted almonds. Refrigerate leftovers.

Makes 4 servings.

BLUEBERRY PRETZEL SQUARES

A gelatin, cream cheese, strawberry, blueberry salad...or dessert.

Crust
1½ cups finely crushed pretzels
¼ cup granulated sugar
⅔ cup melted butter

Filling
2 8-ounce packages cream cheese, softened
¾ cup granulated sugar
1 teaspoon pure vanilla extract
1 8-ounce container frozen non-dairy whipped topping, thawed

2 cups boiling water
1 6-ounce package strawberry flavor gelatin mix
1 cup frozen blueberries
1 16-ounce package frozen strawberries

Preheat oven to 350°.
Mix all crust ingredients. Press firmly onto bottom of a 13x9-inch baking dish. Bake 8 minutes. Cool completely.

Beat cream cheese, sugar and vanilla until smooth. Fold in whipped topping. Spread over crust. Refrigerate and chill until set. Sprinkle blueberries evenly over cheese layer. Stir boiling water into gelatin mix until dissolved. Add frozen strawberries; stir until berries are thawed. Pour mixture over cream cheese layer. Refrigerate until firm. Cut into squares. Garnish with additional whipped topping if desired. Store in refrigerator.

Makes 16 servings.

BLUEBERRY SIX-CUP SALAD

Easy and delicious.

1 cup blueberries
1 cup pineapple chunks
1 cup mandarin oranges
1 cup coconut
1 cup miniature marshmallows
1 cup dairy sour cream

Mix all ingredients in a glass serving bowl. Refrigerate and chill overnight.
Store any leftovers in refrigerator.

Makes 6 cups.

good!.   *8.20.08*

BLUEBERRY TORTELLINI SALAD

Serve this pasta fruit salad on a special day.

1 9-ounce package three-cheese tortellini pasta
   (in the freezer case)
1 cup fresh blueberries
1 cup sliced fresh strawberries
1 11-ounce can mandarin orange segments, drained
¾ cup green grapes
¼ cup toasted sliced almonds

Dressing
3 tablespoons granulated sugar
1 tablespoon vinegar
1½ teaspoons fresh lemon juice
¼ teaspoon salt
¼ teaspoon dry mustard
¼ cup olive oil
2 teaspoons poppy seeds

Cook pasta according to package directions; drain and place into a large bowl. Add remaining salad ingredients. Add salad dressing (see directions below); toss lightly. Serve or refrigerate until ready to serve.

Mix first five dressing ingredients. Gradually add olive oil, beating until thick and smooth. Stir in poppy seeds. Cover and refrigerate several hours for best flavor.

Makes 6 servings.

BLUEBERRY-FILLED WATERMELON

Perfect for that backyard picnic.

1 oblong watermelon
3 cups cantaloupe balls
3 cups honeydew melon balls
1 pineapple, peeled, cored and cut into bite-size pieces
2 fresh peaches
2 cups fresh blueberries
2 tablespoons fresh lime juice
3 tablespoons honey
½ cup ginger ale

Cut off lengthwise the top third of watermelon. With a melon ball cutter, scoop balls from larger portion of the watermelon. Remove seeds from balls; place into a bowl and refrigerate. Remove remaining pulp from watermelon; drain. Cut a thin slice from bottom so melon will stand up; refrigerate.

Place cantaloupe, honeydew and pineapple into another bowl; refrigerate.

When ready to serve, peel and slice peaches; place into a large bowl. Add blueberries, drained melon balls and pineapple. Mix lime juice, honey and ginger ale. Add to fruit, and toss to mix well. Spoon fruit into watermelon shell. Refrigerate.

Carve the cut-off top third of watermelon into a handle if desired.

Makes 10 servings.

BLUEBERRY WATERGATE SALAD

Blueberries tucked in the original Watergate salad.

1 3.4-ounce package pistachio flavor instant pudding & pie filling
1 20-ounce can crushed pineapple in juice, undrained
1 cup miniature marshmallows
½ cup chopped pecans
1 cup fresh blueberries, rinsed and patted dry
2 cups thawed non-dairy frozen whipped topping

In a large glass serving bowl, stir pudding mix, pineapple with juice, marshmallows and nuts until well blended. Stir in blueberries. Fold in whipped topping. Chill well. Refrigerate leftovers.

Makes 8 servings.

CARROT-BLUEBERRY SALAD

Freshly grated carrots with fruit in a tangy creamy dressing.

4 medium-size fresh carrots, grated
1 8-ounce can crushed pineapple, drained
1 cup raisins
1 cup flaked coconut
½ cup maraschino cherries, cut up
⅓ cup dried blueberries
1 10-ounce package miniature marshmallows
½ cup mayonnaise
1 tablespoon fresh lemon juice
1 tablespoon orange juice
½ cup whipping cream, whipped

Mix first seven ingredients. Mix mayonnaise, lemon and orange juice; fold in whipped cream. Pour over carrot mixture; toss until coated. Best served immediately. Refrigerate any leftovers.

Makes 10 servings.

CRANBERRY-BLUEBERRY SALAD

A nice molded salad for special days.

8.12.09 – Modify

1 6-ounce package strawberry flavored gelatin
1½ cups boiling water
1 16-ounce can whole berry cranberry sauce
⅓ cup cold water
1 16-ounce can jellied cranberry sauce
1 cup peeled and cored apple, diced
⅔ cup chopped pecans — *CINN Almonds*
½ cup diced celery *CARROT*
⅓ cup dried blueberries
1 8-ounce package cream cheese, cubed *+ Small MERINGUES*
sweetened whipped cream *w/ yogurt + honey sauce*

Dissolve strawberry gelatin with boiling water and stir in whole berry cranberry sauce; pour into a 13x9-inch glass dish or a mold. Refrigerate and chill until partially set, but not firm.

Stir in ⅓ cup cold water. Stir in remaining ingredients. Chill in freezer one hour; remove from freezer and immediately refrigerate. When serving, top with sweetened whipped cream as desired. Store leftovers in refrigerator.

Makes 12 servings.

FRESH BLUEBERRY CHICKEN SALAD

A colorful salad dressed with lemon yogurt.

¾ **cup lemon yogurt**
3 tablespoons mayonnaise
1 teaspoon salt
⅛ **teaspoon ground white pepper**
2 cups cubed cooked chicken breast
½ **cup thinly sliced green onions**
¾ **cup diagonally sliced celery**
½ **cup diced sweet red bell pepper**
2 cups blueberries, divided
mixed crisp salad greens

In a glass serving bowl, mix yogurt, mayonnaise, salt and pepper until well blended. Add chicken, green onions, celery and bell pepper. Stir to mix well. Fold in 1½ cups blueberries. Cover and chill 30 minutes.

Serve over salad greens. Garnish with ½ cup blueberries. Refrigerate leftovers.

Makes 4 servings.

BLUEBERRY-COCONUT SOUP

Coconut milk, toasted coconut with a touch of lime.

3 cups blueberries, whole or pureed
¾ cup granulated sugar
½ cup water
grated rind of 1 fresh lime
¼ cup fresh lime juice
1 15-ounce can light coconut milk
⅓ cup flaked coconut, toasted

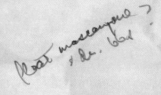

In a saucepan, mix blueberries, sugar, water, lime rind and lime juice. Bring to a boil; reduce heat and simmer 10 minutes. Pour mixture into a large bowl; chill.

Using a wire whisk, whisk coconut milk until smooth; stir into chilled soup. Serve; garnish each bowl with toasted coconut. Store leftovers in refrigerator.

Makes 6 servings.

BLUEBERRY-RASPBERRY SWIRL SOUP

Share a bowl with someone special.

1¼ cups fresh blueberries, divided
½ cup buttermilk
½ cup plain yogurt
1 10-ounce package unsweetened frozen raspberries, thawed
½ cup vanilla-flavored yogurt

Puree 1 cup blueberries in a blender or food processor. Strain to remove skins. Place strained berries in a bowl; stir in buttermilk and plain yogurt. Chill well.

Strain raspberries to remove seeds; discard seeds. Place strained raspberries in a bowl; stir in vanilla-flavored yogurt. Chill well.

When serving, spoon equal amounts of blueberry mixture into 2 bowls. Spoon equal amounts of raspberry mixture into both bowls, placing mixture to one side of the blueberry mixture. Using tip of a knife, swirl mixtures.

Garnish with remaining blueberries. Serve or refrigerate.

Makes 2 servings.

OLD NORWAY BLUEBERRY SOUP

Garnished with fresh mint...you bet.

1 envelope unflavored gelatin
¼ cup cold water
4 cups fresh orange juice
3 tablespoons fresh lemon juice
¼ cup granulated sugar
⅛ teaspoon ground cinnamon
2 cups fresh blueberries
fresh chopped mint

In a small cup, soften gelatin in cold water; place cup in a pan of hot water; stir until dissolved. Pour mixture into a bowl. Stir in juices, sugar and cinnamon until will blended. Stir in blueberries. Chill to serve. Garnish with fresh chopped mint when serving. Store in refrigerator.

Makes 6 servings.

Beverages
Miscellaneous

BLUEBERRY-BANANA SMOOTHIE

No monkey business...it's good!

1 cup fresh blueberries
1 ripe banana, peeled and sliced
½ cup fresh orange juice
2 goodly scoops frozen vanilla yogurt
½ cup ice

In a blender, whirl all ingredients until smooth. Serve immediately in chilled glasses, or freeze.

Make 2 servings.

BLUEBERRY FROSTY

A smooth treat.

2 cups blueberries
1 cup apple juice
1 cup frozen vanilla yogurt
½ cup milk
¾ teaspoon ground cinnamon
¼ teaspoon pure vanilla extract

In a blender or food processor, whirl all ingredients until smooth. Serve immediately or freeze.

Makes about 4 cups.

BLUEBERRY LEMONADE

A refreshing drink.

3 cups blueberries
½ cup granulated sugar, or as desired
1 cup fresh lemon juice
3 cups cold water
ice cubes

In a blender, puree blueberries; strain through a fine sieve into a serving pitcher. Add sugar, lemon juice and water. Stir well. Serve over ice cubes in large glasses. Refrigerate leftovers.

Makes 4 servings.

BLUEBERRY-ORANGE WHIRL

Swirled with vanilla yogurt.

2½ cups fresh blueberries
1 8-ounce container low-fat vanilla yogurt
½ cup fresh orange juice
½ cup milk
1 teaspoon pure vanilla extract

In a blender, whirl all ingredients until smooth. Serve in chilled glasses immediately.

Makes 4 servings.

BLUEBERRY-PINEAPPLE SMOOTHIE

Good sipping.

2 cups blueberries
1 8-ounce container vanilla flavor yogurt
1 cup whole milk
1 6-ounce can unsweetened pineapple juice
3 tablespoons honey
1½ cups ice cubes

In a blender, whirl all ingredients except ice until smooth. Add ice cubes a few at a time; whirl until finely crushed. Serve.

Makes about 5 cups.

BLUEBERRY PURPLE PUNCH

Strawberries and frozen lemonade adds to the "punch."

3 cups fresh blueberries
2 cups granulated sugar
2 10-ounce packages frozen strawberries, thawed
2 quarts ginger ale, chilled
1 6-ounce can frozen lemonade, slightly thawed

In a saucepan, stir and cook blueberries and sugar for 5 minutes.

Add strawberries; cook and stir 5 minutes. Strain over a bowl; chill; discard pulp. Add ginger ale and lemonade. Serve over crushed ice. Refrigerate.

Makes about 12 servings.

ICE CREAM BLUEBERRY SMOOTHIE

Use regular or low-fat ice cream and yogurt in this delicious smoothie.

1 cup blueberries, do not thaw if using frozen berries
1 cup vanilla ice cream
¼ cup vanilla yogurt
½ cup chopped canned peaches
½ cup unsweetened pineapple juice

In a blender, whirl all ingredients until smooth. Freeze leftovers.

Makes 2 servings.

TASTY BLUEBERRY TREAT

Garnish with fresh sliced strawberries when serving.

2 8-ounce cans crushed pineapple, drained
2 ripe bananas, sliced
2 cups milk
2 cups fresh or frozen blueberries

In a blender or food processor, whirl all ingredients until thick and smooth. Serve immediately.

Makes 6 servings.

BLUEBERRY FILLING

Simple and delicious.

¾ cup granulated sugar
2 tablespoons cornstarch
⅛ teaspoon salt
¼ cup cold water
¼ cup light corn syrup
4½ cups blueberries, fresh or frozen
1 teaspoon fresh lemon juice
1 teaspoon pure vanilla extract

In a heavy 3-quart saucepan, mix sugar, cornstarch and salt. Stir in water until smooth. Stir in corn syrup and blueberries; cook over medium-low heat until bubbly and thickened, about 4 minutes for fresh, but a little longer if using frozen berries. Stir in lemon juice and vanilla. Spoon mixture into a bowl. Cover and refrigerate if not using immediately.

Makes about 2 cups.

BLUEBERRY SAUCE

Delicate flavor.

⅓ cup granulated sugar
4 teaspoons cornstarch
⅛ teaspoon salt
⅛ teaspoon ground cinnamon
½ cup water
½ teaspoon fresh lemon juice
½ teaspoon pure vanilla extract
2½ cups fresh blueberries

In a saucepan, mix sugar, cornstarch, salt and cinnamon. Stir in water and lemon juice. Bring to a boil, over medium-high heat, stirring constantly; cook and stir 1 minute. Stir in vanilla and blueberries; cook about 1 minute. Serve warm or at room temperature. Cover and store in refrigerator.

Makes about 2½ cups.

BLUEBERRY-ORANGE TOPPING

Good over waffles.

3 tablespoons granulated sugar
1 tablespoon cornstarch
¼ teaspoon salt
⅛ teaspoon ground nutmeg
¼ cup fresh orange juice
¼ cup water
1 cup blueberries, fresh or frozen
1 cup orange sections, (about 2 oranges), membranes removed
½ teaspoon pure vanilla extract

Mix sugar, cornstarch, salt and nutmeg; set aside.

In a saucepan, bring orange juice and water to a boil. Add blueberries and orange sections; return to a boil. Reduce heat; cook 3 minutes, or a little longer if blueberries are frozen. Stir in vanilla. Add sugar mixture, stirring and cooking constantly until thickened, about 1 minute.

Serve warm or chilled. Store in refrigerator.

Makes 2 cups.

BLUEBERRY-PINEAPPLE TOPPING

Good over pound cake, ice cream and other good things.

1 8-ounce can crushed pineapple
¼ cup pineapple preserves
1 cup blueberries

In a small saucepan, bring pineapple and preserves to a boil over medium heat. Stir in blueberries; remove from heat. Spoon into a bowl. Serve at room temperature or chilled. Store in refrigerator.

Makes 1½ cups.

BLUEBERRY-BANANA TOPPING

Serve this tasty topping over crisp waffles.

1 tablespoon butter
½ cup broken pecan pieces
1 cup maple syrup
1 ripe banana, cut into ½-inch slices
1 cup fresh blueberries

In a saucepan, mix butter and pecans; stir and cook over medium heat 2 minutes. Reduce heat. Add syrup, bananas and blueberries; simmer 3 minutes. Serve warm. Refrigerate leftovers.

Makes about 2 cups.

BLUEBERRY SYRUP

Serve this deep blue colored syrup over favorite pancakes.

5 cups fresh blueberries
3 cups granulated sugar
¾ cup water
1 tablespoon fresh lemon juice
½ teaspoon pure vanilla extract

In a large heavy saucepan, mix blueberries and sugar; let stand 1 hour. Add water and lemon juice; bring to a boil over high heat. Skim off foam. Reduce heat; simmer until mixture thickens, about 15 minutes. Stir in vanilla. Remove from heat; strain through a fine sieve. Cool. Pour into a glass container. Store in refrigerator.

Makes about 2 cups.

BLUEBERRY CINNAMON SYRUP

Serve warm over favorite pancakes, French toast or waffles.

1 cup pure maple syrup
2 cups fresh blueberries
¼ teaspoon ground cinnamon, or to taste

In a saucepan, heat syrup over medium heat. Stir in blueberries; simmer 3 minutes. Pour mixture through a sieve, over a bowl, pressing blueberries with back of a large spoon to extract juice; discard pulp. Stir in cinnamon. Pour mixture into a serving pitcher. Serve warm. Refrigerate leftovers.

Makes about 1½ cups.

BLUEBERRY JAM

Flavorful spread for that breakfast toast.

6 cups blueberries
2 tablespoons lemon juice
½ teaspoon ground cinnamon
¼ teaspoon ground allspice
⅛ teaspoon ground cloves, scant
7 cups granulated sugar
1 6-ounce package liquid fruit pectin (2 foil pouches)

In a large heavy saucepan, crush blueberries. Add lemon juice, cinnamon, allspice and cloves; mix well. Stir in sugar.

Bring to a full rolling boil, stirring constantly. Stir in pectin. Return to a full rolling boil; boil 1 minute, stirring constantly. Remove from heat. Immediately skim off foam with a large spoon.

Ladle at once into hot sterilized jars, leaving ¼ inch headspace. Adjust lids. Process in a boiling-water canner bath for 5 minutes. Remove from bath.

Makes 9 half-pints.

MICROWAVE BLUEBERRY JAM

Great on those homemade biscuits.

1 cup mashed fresh blueberries
¾ cup granulated sugar
¼ teaspoon ground cinnamon
2 teaspoons fresh lemon juice
¼ teaspoon butter

In a 2-quart microwave-safe casserole, mix all ingredients.

Microwave on 100% power (high) for 8–9 minutes or until mixture thickens and is reduced to about 1 cup, stirring every 2 minutes. Cool. If jam become too stiff, add a teaspoon of water at a time to thin. Cover and store in refrigerator.

Makes about 1 cup.

BLUEBERRY MORNING MIX

Pack some in a small plastic food bag for a healthy on-the-go breakfast, or serve as a party mix to drop-in company.

3 cups corn chex cereal
3 cups rice chex cereal
3 cups wheat chex cereal
1 cup sliced almonds
1 cup broken pecan pieces
⅓ cup butter or margarine, melted
⅓ cup brown sugar, packed
⅓ cup frozen orange juice concentrate, thawed
½ cup dried blueberries
½ cup dried cranberries
½ cup raisins

Preheat oven to 300°.
Mix cereals and nuts; set aside.

In a microwave-safe bowl, microwave butter, sugar and orange juice uncovered on high for 30 seconds; stir well. Pour mixture over cereal mixture. Stir until evenly coated. Pour into a large roasting pan.

Bake uncovered 30 minutes, stirring after 15 minutes. Remove from oven; immediately stir in blueberries, cranberries and raisins. Cool completely. Store in an airtight container or plastic food storage bag.

Makes about 12 cups.

BLUEBERRY GRANOLA

A breakfast treat.

4 cups quick-cooking oatmeal, uncooked
1 cup flaked coconut
½ cup chopped walnuts
½ cup chopped pecans
¼ cup chopped almonds
1 cup dried blueberries
½ cup dried cranberries
½ cup dried cherries, chopped
½ cup all-bran cereal
¼ cup sesame seeds
½ cup corn oil
½ cup maple syrup
½ teaspoon pure vanilla extract
¼ teaspoon salt

Preheat oven to 325°.
Mix the first ten ingredients.

Stir corn oil, syrup, vanilla and salt; spoon over the first mixture and toss until coated. Spread in an even layer in a greased 15x10x1-inch baking pan. Bake 30–35 minutes until granola is lightly browned. Stir mixture gently after 20 minutes baking.

Remove from oven. Immediately turn out onto another large baking sheet. Cool completely. Store in plastic food bags at room temperature no longer than 2 weeks; freeze for longer storage.

Makes about 10 cups.

TRAIL MIX WITH BLUEBERRIES

A tasty snack.

⅓ cup margarine, melted
¼ cup honey
3 tablespoons brown sugar
3 cups quick-cooking oatmeal, uncooked
½ cup wheat bran cereal
¼ cup raw sunflower seeds, shelled
1 teaspoon ground cinnamon
⅓ cup wheat germ
⅓ cup sliced almonds
⅓ cup pecan pieces
⅓ cup walnut pieces
⅓ cup dried apple bits
⅓ cup shredded coconut
1 teaspoon pure vanilla extract
½ teaspoon almond extract
¾ cup dried blueberries

Preheat oven to 350°.
In a 13x9-inch baking pan, stir margarine, honey and brown sugar.

Mix oatmeal, cereal, sunflower seeds and cinnamon; stir into first mixture.
Bake 15 minutes, stirring every 5 minutes. Stir in remaining ingredients
except blueberries; bake 10 minutes or until golden brown. Remove from
oven and immediately stir in blueberries. Cool completely before storing.

Makes about 6 cups.

About the Author

Theresa Millang is a popular and versatile cookbook author. She has written successful cookbooks on muffins, brownies, pies, cookies, cheesecake, casseroles, and several on Cajun cooking. She has cooked on television, and contributed many recipes to food articles throughout the U.S.A..

Theresa's Other Cookbooks
I Love Cheesecake
I Love Pies You Don't Bake
The Muffins Are Coming

Theresa's Other Current Cookbooks
The Best of Cajun-Creole Recipes
The Best of Chili Recipes
The Great Minnesota Hot Dish